More Praise for
MOTHERLAND: WRITINGS BY IRISH AMERICAN WOMEN ABOUT MOTHERS AND DAUGHTERS

"A wonderfully rich book. It reminds me of a buffet table with many fine foods for us to try. . . . Kearns has done Irish Americans a great service because she edited this collection of graceful and insightful works." —*Irish American*

"Kearns leaves it unquestionable that the literary pedigree of Irish-American women is strong and impressive." —*Booklist*

"Heartfelt . . . humorous . . . philosophical . . . [Kearns creates] a final product which truly reflects issues, desires, and realities in women's lives, past and present, Irish, Irish-American, and universal." —*Irish Edition*

"[A] thoughtful collection. . . . Kearns has done an exemplary job of assembling this anthology." —*Publishers Weekly*

Motherland

ALSO BY CALEDONIA KEARNS

Cabbage and Bones: An Anthology of Irish American Women's Fiction

Motherland

Writings by Irish American Women About Mothers and Daughters

Edited and with an Introduction by
Caledonia Kearns

Perennial
An Imprint of HarperCollins*Publishers*

A hardcover edition of this book was published in 1999 by William Morrow and Company, Inc.

MOTHERLAND. Copyright © 1999 by Caledonia Kearns. All rights reserved. Printed in the United States of America. No part of this book may be used or reproduced in any matter whatsoever without written permission except in the case of brief quotations embodied in critical articles and reviews. For information address HarperCollins Publishers Inc., 10 East 53rd Street, New York, NY 10022.

HarperCollins books may be purchased for educational, business, or sales promotional use. For information please write: Special Markets Department, HarperCollins Publishers Inc., 10 East 53rd Street, New York, NY 10022.

First Perennial edition published 2000.

Designed by Trina Stahl

The Library of Congress has catalogued the hardcover edition as follows:

Kearns, Caledonia.
    Motherland : writings by Irish American women about mothers and daughters / Caledonia Kearns. — 1st ed.
        p.   cm.
    ISBN 0-688-16565-6 (acid-free paper)
        1. Mothers and daughters—Fiction.   2. American prose literature—Irish American authors. 3. American prose literature—Women authors. 4. Irish American women—Fiction. 5. Mother and child—Fiction. 6. Women—Ireland—Fiction. 7. Motherhood—Fiction. 8. Motherhood. 9. Mothers. I. Kearns, Caledonia.
PS648.M59M57   1999
810.8'03520431—dc21   98-33901
                                    CIP

ISBN 0-688-17586-4 (pbk.)

00 01 02 03 04 ❖/RRD 10 9 8 7 6 5 4 3 2 1

For my mother,
Marjorie Farrell,
who shares her stories
and has passed on her
faith in the word

and for Miguel Martinez
with all my heart

Contents

Contents

Contents

Contents

Acknowledgments

I T DOES TAKE a village to raise a child and many women along with my mother mothered me. My godmother, Monica Cornell, cared for my infant self as if I were her own. Ann McGlinchy Grady always had a place ready for me at her table. I thank Judy Luce for her open heart and Cathy Schwartz for her willing ear and her trust. My aunt Leslie Baker throughout my childhood supported me and my mother and for this we were blessed. My mother-in-law, Mary Alice Riddle Martinez, and the Riddle sisters welcomed me into their family with open arms.

Victoria Sanders, my agent, teaches me how to take chances and rocks the house, and my editor, Meaghan Dowling, is a real gem who has unfailingly supported my efforts. This book would not exist without them and I am grateful for their hard work. I also thank Kelli Martin at Morrow for her kind assistance. Liza Featherstone is a true friend and one-woman support system and my sisters, the Grady girls, are always wonderfully there. The staff and students at Begin Employment, and especially Kerry Herlihy, lifted me up when I needed it and taught me how to breathe.

While this book is a tribute to mothers, I would like to praise a few men: my uncles John Aloysius Farrell, writer and role model, and Jock Baker, possessor of unflagging joie de vivre. Dorchester dads Francis Grady and Bob Schwartz took care of me. Last but not least, my grandfather John Aloysius Farrell, Sr., has always looked out for me and I love him dearly.

I thank all of my contributors for their stories and am delighted by their collective voice. They remind me that work, writing, and motherhood are part of the same whole.

My mother Marjorie Farrell's imprint is on every page. Our discussions about women and Ireland have been invaluable. She is a friend and colleague who has seen me through. I have always admired women like her who have raised children alone. I raise my glass to her, Joan and Mary Farrell, Adele Powers Bohne, Marie Reilly, Kathleen Shaw, and countless others.

Finally, although our grandmother was lost to us before we were born, she is at the center of my musings about Ireland. This is for my cousins Caitlin Christine Farrell and John Aloysius Farrell (the fifth!). Here's to the part of her that lives within.

Introduction

BY CALEDONIA KEARNS

Ireland has always been a woman, a womb, a cave, a cow, a Rosaleen,
a sow, a bride, a harlot, and, of course, the gaunt Hag of Beare.
—EDNA O'BRIEN FROM *Mother Ireland*

M Y GRANDMOTHER AND great-grandmother passed down
a profound sense of their Irish identity to my mother and,
in turn, to me without ever stepping foot on Irish soil. For them,
Ireland was an idealized place where *their* grandmothers and great-
grandmothers came from. The sense of identity and history I carry
has survived for over a hundred years and is five generations old.
Ireland is our motherland.

At the same time we carry an idyllic vision of this motherland,
we are also aware of Ireland's difficult history. She has been invaded
and betrayed. She is the mother of a people she has never been
able to fully care for; the diaspora is a result of her suffering.
Mother Ireland has been abandoned, and fallen victim to famine.
Her children have wandered—they have crossed oceans because
she could not feed them.

This archetypal image of a female Ireland has pervaded Irish literature. In song, poetry, and legend, the image persists. From the ninth-century poem "The Hag of Beare" through Yeats to Seamus Heaney, Ireland has been written about by countless male poets. Yeats called her Cathleen ni Houlihan, in song she is Dark Rosaleen—a woman in relation to men who are either her lovers or her sons. Yet what about her daughters?

After the Famine, land was inherited by a single son, which left Irish daughters bereft and at the mercy of their fathers or their brothers. One of the basic facts of Irish immigration to the United States is that women emigrated in larger numbers than men. The solid prospect of domestic work in the United States was enticing. When they left, daughters left for good. Their mothers keened and held wakes for the living.

Just as daughters need to leave their mothers to discover themselves, Irish daughters left their mothers and their motherland to fend for themselves. Given the pain of this separation, it is fitting that John Boyle O'Reilly referred to the Atlantic Ocean as a "bowl of tears."

It is a strange motherland in which the mother does not tell her own story. Eavan Boland in her essay "A Kind of Scar" describes her need to write herself into the tradition of Irish poetry because, until the twentieth century, male poets dominated Irish writing. Their writing about Ireland as a woman appropriated the voice of the female poet so that it was a struggle for Irish women to claim a voice of their own. It also becomes important to ask: what then is the role of the Irish American woman writer, and how does she define her motherland as well as herself?

I am the great-great-granddaughter of Mary McDermott from

Elphin, County Roscommon. She left Ireland alone in 1877 at twelve years of age to come to the States, never to return. To me, Ireland is a touchstone. I am able to place myself in the history of the United States by looking at the events in Irish history that caused emigration. I can also place Mary McDermott into that history. My mother and I went to Elphin last summer to see how far Mary McDermott traveled. It is peculiar to be Irish American in Ireland—embarrassed by the search for a place in a country that often makes fun of the Yanks who come looking for Paddy, or Mary as in our case. Are we really who we think we are?

THE WRITINGS IN THIS collection, fiction and nonfiction, are written from the perspectives of Irish American mothers and daughters. I believe that women writers, all women writers, need to write themselves into history. To assert their voices, to claim the pen as their own, female experience as theirs to define. Some of the selections are heartrending: Mary Cantwell's writing about a difficult birth, the dilemmas Mary Gordon faces caring for her aging mother; some are humorous: M.F.K. Fisher's portrait of her mother and Jean Kerr's wanting her visiting adult children to treat her as a hostess. Others are political, Elizabeth Gurley Flynn, a labor leader, writes of her mother's activism, a precursor to her own. Mary Doyle Curran also writes of her mother's politics, while Mother Jones is included as the "mother" of the American labor movement. Considering that she lost four of her children and her husband in a fever epidemic, it makes sense that she was later willing to risk her own life for the improved working conditions of others—she had nothing left to lose. The birth control activist

Margaret Sanger (née Higgins) is also included. While the motives of her population control campaign have been questioned, she was clearly ahead of her time, writing extensively on what she felt to be the ideal conditions of motherhood.

As in *Cabbage and Bones: An Anthology of Irish American Women's Fiction*, I have endeavored to include women whose work is now out of print or in danger of being forgotten. Ellin Mackay Berlin, Irving Berlin's wife of more than sixty years, was a well-known novelist in her time, and *Lace Curtain*, the story of the well-to-do Reardon family and their experience with their Protestant neighbors, has been all but lost. This excerpt from *Lace Curtain* has a young girl discovering her connection to the Blessed Mother. Elizabeth Gurley Flynn's *The Rebel Girl* is a wonderful and useful history of a political activist. Maeve Brennan was a longtime writer for *The New Yorker* whose stories were collected posthumously by Houghton Mifflin. She died penniless in 1993 at age seventy-six after spending time in and out of hospitals because of mental instability. Brennan left Ireland and lived in the States from the time she was seventeen years old, yet all of her fiction is set in Ireland.

What makes this collection of writing Irish American besides the fact that the writing of Irish American women is preoccupied with mothers? Helena Mulkerns, also Irish born, writes of leaving her mother in Ireland as she lives her life in the United States. Kerry Herlihy's mother and birthmother are both Irish American, and while there is no singular Irish American experience, their shared culture connects them. Mother Jones is intriguing in that on the very first page of her autobiography she explicitly draws parallels between her Irishness and her activism. The selection from Lisa Carey's *The Mermaids Singing* examines the relationship of three generations of women to the United States and Ireland.

I don't think it is fair to say that Irish American women write to discover their motherland. I will say that the more generationally removed from Ireland, the easier it becomes to construct an idealized image of her. I am not Irish—my passport certifies that I am an American citizen—yet where my ancestors came from matters to me. I need to identify myself as Irish and American. I find in the writing of Irish American women connections between my own experience and the experience of others. I cannot think of a better way to explore identity than through their stories. The work included here is deeply personal. The nonfiction is explicitly an exploration of the self, while the fiction is an opportunity to imagine another way of being.

At the end of "A Kind of Scar," Eavan Boland writes, "If a poet does not tell the truth about time, her or his work will not survive it." My hope is that the works included here speak their own truth about identity, motherhood, and family and will do more than survive. Within these pages I have endeavored to write honestly about my own mother, and I chose these pieces, however varied, because there was something in them that rang true. Whether written by mothers or daughters, they are an effort to explore what motherhood can be and how daughters experience their mothers. Ultimately, this collection, while grounded in the Irish American, is universal. It is my deepest wish that these selections will give a further voice to the experience of all American mothers and daughters.

The Bonesetter

Carolyn Curtin Alessio

Until I was twelve, I considered my mother an ethnic renegade. She'd repudiated her Irish-immigrant parents in a single, flagrant act, by marrying a young engineer by the name of Sergio Antonio Alessio. My pride in my mother's daring was great, and for years, when I signed my full name, I often paused, considering all the Irish surnames I might have had if my mother had complied with tradition and added to Curtin, her maiden name, a last name that might have begun and not ended with *O*.

In assuming my mother's heroism, however, I overlooked several key factors which suggested that perhaps my parents were not such an unlikely match: both were the children of European immigrants (my mother's parents hailed from County Limerick, my father's parents from Bassano del Grappa in Northern Italy); both were avid readers and had put themselves through college, and both were practicing Roman Catholics. But in my irrepressible ability to romanticize, I reveled in the improbability of their union. At Sunday Mass, when the priest spoke in his sermon of "mixed" marriages—ironically, he meant Catholic and Protestant—I privately substituted Irish and Italian. Even looking in the mirror took on a sort of mystique: though I have my father's dark eyes and ability to tan, my face has always been so freckled as to resemble an experiment in pointillism.

I learned many Irish customs and habits from my mother's mother, Mary O'Connor Curtin. Though it seemed incongruous to me, my mother's family had not renounced her for her marital defection: perhaps they viewed it as an inevitable dilution of the gene pool, or yet another trial in the family's narrative. In any event, I often wound up with my mother in Grandma Curtin's dim kitchen, in a Depression-era bungalow in a predominantly Irish neighborhood on the West Side of Chicago.

Sipping tea from Beleek china dotted with pale shamrocks, we'd listen to scratchy recordings of Irish tenor John McCormick, or sometimes, the more modern Clancy Brothers who cavorted and sang such whimsical numbers as "The Boys Won't Leave the Girls Alone." In that house on Massasoit Street, my grandmother read us obituaries from the *Tribune* (focusing on the deceased with Irish names), smoked, and imparted folk beliefs. For example, she told us that a bird lingering on the roof of one's house foretold certain death. And always, my grandmother told stories from the Old Country, a place that she always called "back home," though she'd left it at age sixteen to come to the States, where she took a job as a live-in nanny for a wealthy German family.

Hardship and hyperbole were mainstays in my grandmother's tales. In one story that she repeated often, her mother broke her leg while working the family's farm. There were seven children then, a baby on the way, and a husband who wasn't always reliable. At this point in the story, my grandmother would pause and purse her lips, as though considering the pathos of the situation for the first time. Cigarette smoke rose up around her in tiny, gray cyclones. I would try to imagine my grandmother's family home, her ailing mother, her youngest sister Bridie, who later would die in my grandmother's arms. All I could summon up, though, was the damp Chicago kitchen in which we sat, sipping tea and listening. "But the Bonesetter came," my grandmother would say, leaning forward, "the Bonesetter came and fixed Ma's leg."

We were never certain who the Bonesetter was—a combination chiropractor and orthopedist, or even some kind of Celtic shaman. My grandmother took it for granted that we would understand the power of such a person. Further, she seemed to believe that answering petty inquiries about his profession might somehow weaken the Bonesetter's storied capabilities. Years later, I would read of a bonesetter in *Ulysses*, an old lady's "medicineman," but somehow I could not connect this definition with the semimythical hero of my grandmother's tales.

Despite the Bonesetter's ability to mitigate suffering, the majority of my grandmother's tales took on a maudlin twist, evolving into tales of misplaced love and longing, of dissipation and the failure to combat the cruelty of the surrounding world. Children, like her infant sister, died of quick, feverish illnesses; women over forty married out of desperation and bore children who were "never quite right." These tragedies were not confined to Ireland, however, but seemed to follow the immigrants to the States, where middle-aged men would keel over from heart attacks in pubs, priests would begin to spit up blood while saying a funeral mass, young women would spend their earnings on war bonds, only to receive word that their fiancés and their brothers had died overseas.

It would be years before I would read Joyce, Yeats, Frank O'Connor and Flannery O'Connor, but I learned early from my grandmother's heartbreaking stories a sense of Irishness that I would later translate—however illogically—into my own sense of complicity in the disappointing of God. As a child, however, I knew only that I experienced a curious mixture of yearning and relief when my grandmother would finish her stories for the day, and bid us "Safe Home" as she waved from the front porch, a cigarette still burning in her hand.

Predictably, it was my grandmother, not my mother, who told me about my mother's prophetic dream. One night during the late fifties in the Chicago house, my mother was awakened by a dream. A pleading, raspy voice was calling "Ma" again and again. Startled awake, my mother awoke her own mother, who assured her that nothing was wrong. The next morning, they received word from Ireland that Brigit McNamara O'Connor, my mother's grandmother, had passed away during the night.

ONE NIGHT DURING THE summer I was twelve, my mother and I played Trivial Pursuit. My father and younger sister had gone for a bike ride and I was pleased and a bit smug at the prospect of having my mother's undivided attention. If the game went well, I planned to tell her about a new crush of mine, a boy who could play the clarinet so bewitchingly that a group of us sometimes gathered around the practice rooms at school to listen.

The game was barely underway. My mother had landed on Brown, our favorite category, "Arts & Literature." I reached for the card, located the question, and read, "In the play, 'Dial "M" for Murder,' where was the key hidden?"

This one was easy. I knew that Hitchcock had made this play into a movie, and Grace Kelly had starred in it. My mother loved Grace Kelly, or Princess Grace, as she called her.

"Mom," I said. I waited, looked around at the family room's paneled walls, then turned back to my mother. Her face was pale, I saw, and her freckles were darker than usual.

"Mom? Are you tired?"

"I don't know," she said. "A little."

"Should we watch TV?"

"I'm sorry," my mother said. "I'm thinking of a man I saw that movie with. Jim O'Flaherty. His parents, Rose and Fip, lived down the block from us."

This was a name I had never heard her mention before. "Was he your boyfriend?" I said. "Did you go on dates?"

"We'd go dancing and to the show. Hitchcock was one of his favorites."

"Was he good-looking?"

"Black curly hair," my mother said. "Tall."

I didn't often get to talk to my mother on this level. "Did you kiss him?"

"It was innocent back then," my mother said. "He had a car, but we'd only drive places in it."

I still was not convinced he had existed. "What was his job?"

"Schoolteacher," my mother said. "For a while he'd worked in personnel at a factory downtown, but the bosses made him turn away Blacks. Jim hated it so he went back to school and became a teacher. Sixth grade."

A dark thought occurred to me. "Did he know Dad?"

"No," my mother said, gazing at the wall behind me. "Jim died four years before I met your father. Our last date was two nights before Jim died. June 15, 1954. We went to the Chicago Theater to see 'Dial M for Murder.' "

I waited, and in a moment, she continued. "Ray Milland starred with Grace Kelly. I later read that they'd had an affair while they were filming it, but nobody seemed to know that then.

"After the movie, when we went out to the car, a bird was perched on its roof. Jim held out his finger, but the bird wouldn't budge. Finally we got in the car and drove off."

I struggled not to ask the next question, but I had already heard too much: "How did he die?"

"Car accident," my mother said. "He and two pals were going on a driving trip out East, and somewhere in Ohio, Jim fell asleep at the wheel. They drove into a pole and it crushed him and one of his friends. Jim was twenty-four."

I shifted position and my knee grazed the gameboard, knocking off one of the plastic pies. My chest felt tight inside; I was flooded with sorrow and shame.

"I never told my mother this," my mother said, "but at the funeral, Jim's sister told me he'd tried to call me before he left on the trip. But the line was busy—my mother had been on the phone a long time that night."

"Did you love him?" I asked. "Did you want to marry him?"

My mother hesitated. "I was backward then," she said. "I was working in a steno pool and hadn't even thought about college yet.

I think," she said, looking at me, "I think he would've tired of me after a while."

I sat back, feeling enormously cheated by this answer; suddenly, my mother had betrayed both my romantic nature and the long-held belief that she had spent her early twenties forging a career and waiting to meet my father. Or at least, that she had tolerated other suitors until she discovered one whose family didn't eat soda bread and hold wedding receptions in basements that lasted all night, often into Sunday morning, at which point everyone would troop down the block to sunrise Mass. In my personal revisionist history, I had imagined my mother longing for supper-table conversation that floated around her in mellifluous, Mediterranean syllables, words she couldn't understand, but relished as foreign while she dipped her breadstick into a wine glass. This was my renegade version of my mother: an enterprising young woman determined to divert or at least complicate her own ethnic and cultural road. How, I wondered, could she have been someone who held hands at a Hitchcock movie with a young man who taught sixth graders to diagram sentences and held out his finger as a perch for a bird?

Later, I would think that I should have comforted my mother that night, for she had likely not told anyone this story for years. But all I could think about as she talked was, selfishly, that I had been a product more of chance than intention; perhaps my mother's first dating impulse had not been to rebel. Even later, when she married an Italian, wasn't he, too, a gentle man who made frequent visits to his elderly mother, a superstitious woman who often spoke of "malocchio" or the Evil Eye?

I wish I could say that I sympathized with my mother that night. Compassion, Flannery O'Connor once wrote, is a word that sounds good on anyone's lips. Years later, I would think of that night and the way my lips had failed to form any response to my mother's tale other than detached, factual questions, and a final, surly muteness. If she could not muster up fervor for a long-ago love, I reasoned, how could she understand my ardor for a thirteen-year-old clarinetist who wore skinny ties and smiled at me in the cafeteria? I sat there in the darkening family room, bitter, and embarrassed by my presumptions.

We did not resume the game that night. Soon, from the driveway we heard the clicking of bikes and the lowering of kickstands. My father and sister had returned from their ride.

"Well," my mother said, "we should clean up."

I flipped over the card in my hand. "The fifth step," I read. "Under the fifth step."

My mother looked at me.

"The key," I said, "was hidden under the fifth step." I handed my mother the card.

She studied it. "Yes," she said, then handed it back to me.

I returned the card to the pile and considered clearing the board. My mother got up and began to close the curtains, pausing between windows as my father's voice filled the hallway above us.

from *Lace Curtain*

Ellin Mackay Berlin

V ERONICA REARDON AND Lucy Verity sat on the terrace
steps. The sun was still high in the long June afternoon, but
the children's day was ending. Above the wall, on the terrace,
Nanny was pushing Vincent's carriage slowly toward the front
door. Lucy's Mademoiselle was saying good-by. It was the end of
the day for Veronica but not for the older ones. She watched
them walking through the trees. Frank and Rita and Bernardine
and their friends came first. Jenny and Donald Moore lagged behind the others. The girls wore bright sweaters and white skirts.
They carried tennis rackets. Veronica pushed her brown leather
sandals back and forth in the gravel of the drive. She pulled up
her ribbed brown socks. Bernardine's rose stockings matched her
silk sweater.

"Bernardine's very stylish," Veronica said. "Nanny said so—
'Miss Jane Stylish,' she said. The Jane was in fun."

"Bernardine's pretty," Lucy answered.

"That's what I mean."

Bernardine's prettiness was sheltered from the sun. Only her eyes could be seen above the rosy chiffon veil that was pinned to the brim of her stiff straw hat.

"That's a harem veil," Veronica said, "like in *The Arabian Nights*. I tried it on my hat. It got wet against my mouth. Bernardine was mad."

The older Reardons and their friends were on the steps now. "Hello, Veronica, where are the boys?" They didn't wait for an answer.

"You're lucky, Veronica," Lucy said, "to have a big family."

"I know."

Veronica knew she was luckier than Lucy. Poor Lucy with only her father. Lucy's mother was dead. And that was sad and you couldn't mention it. Poor Lucy. Lucky Veronica, with her big family and her big house. Lucy's house was sort of big but it was built of wood and it didn't look big. It just stretched out as you walked through it. And it was at the foot of a hill and it didn't have a name. It was just called Lucy's or the Veritys'.

Pride's Tower was tall like its name. It stood on a hill and looked down all the way around north, south, east, and west. It was placed neatly, Veronica thought proudly. Tom Pride must have been a proud old man. It was nice to be called Pride and to build a tower on the hilltop.

The Ameses had torn down Tom Pride's tower and they had built a house like a castle and had called it La Colina. Veronica frowned and rejected the name. No one had ever used the foreign name. The country people had continued to call the new house

Pride's Tower. When Veronica's father had bought the place he had given it back its old name.

Veronica touched the warm, white stone of the terrace step with the palm of her hand. The stone is white and beautiful. Daddy was right. Our house is too beautiful for an invented foreign name or for a plain name. Pride's Tower is right for our house. Pride's Tower. It's like a beautiful name from the litany. And it's ours. It's hard to believe that someone else built it and lived in it. But they hardly lived in it. Daddy bought it the year before I was born.

Veronica tried to turn from the difficult thought of time without her. The others remember when I wasn't born. Even Eugene and Jerome say they remember. And Rita and Frank remember very well. Once the Reardons didn't have me and they didn't have Pride's Tower. The tower and I were born to them together. And it feels as though we'd always been.

Veronica looked at her grown-up sisters and brother standing before the tall oak door of Pride's Tower. She drew her sandals back through the gravel and hugged her knees. She smiled at Lucy. "Bernardine's the prettiest and Rita's the oldest and Jenny's the most fun. She and Donald are the nicest to me. They have more time."

"Sure we have time, chicken." Donald tugged one of Veronica's stiff braids. "A little too much if you ask me." Donald took Jenny's hand. "Two more years at school for both of us and then college for me. But maybe we can interrupt the last part of the program."

"Shut up, Donald. They take in everything. Don't you, Miss Innocence?" Jenny patted her small sister's head. "I can remember putting on that blank look and picking up lots of things. Come on, Donald, tea."

"What doesn't she want you to know?" Lucy asked.

"Oh, nothing interesting. Not like Rita and Jim Shea. I heard Nanny say it was going to be announced. That means they're engaged. And we didn't even know Jim Shea till summer before last."

"But what did Jenny not want you to know?"

"Oh, nothing. Everybody knows about her and Donald. They always played together. I can remember that when I was little."

Lucy stood up. "There's the car. I wish the day wasn't over."

Veronica followed Nanny and the baby into the house. She lingered on the landing of the big stairway. Upstairs on the third floor she could hear Eugene and Jerome shouting and slamming the nursery doors. Downstairs she could hear Frank and her sisters. They sang and Jim Shea strummed on his ukulele.

Mrs. Reardon called from the head of the wide stairs. "Is that you, Veronica? Isn't it bath time?"

"Not quite. And, anyway, if you say so Nanny'll let me just wash and have my bath after."

"All right, I'll say so. You seem kind of forlorn standing there between the boys upstairs and the grown-up children below."

"Well, of course, I won't ever be a boy but I'll be grown up and then the boys will play with me more. Rita doesn't even mind Jenny and she's much younger than her. I'm only four years younger than Jerome."

Veronica followed her mother through the library into the west bedroom.

"You'll be grown up, Veronica, and have your summer and your own stylish ways. They won't be the ways of 1916. They'll be your ways."

"A harem veil and a uka—uka—something to play while I'm singing, I mean. . . ."

"They'll play something while you sing, Veronica, and the songs will be the prettiest and the fashions, too. Ukuleles and player pianos you'll have."

"And a weejee board? What's a weejee board, Mother? A boy brought Bernardine one. It's a game with numbers and letters. Lucy and I tried to play it but we didn't know how."

"Have they brought one of those things into the house? Father Janvier will not be pleased. But then he won't know. In my day the parish priest would have known. There wasn't much that Father Murphy didn't know. Yes, the Ouija board's a game, Veronica. A silly game. But it belongs to the summer and it'll be forgotten like the newfangled fashions. The foolish veil that Bernardine wears. As though she could sunburn that white Irish skin of hers."

"Well, can I do what they do? Can I have a Castle bob like Loretta Shea if I want to?"

"You'll do what's done in your time. And you'll not even remember their ways."

"Anyway, I'd rather have diamond pins like yours." Veronica picked up the thick shell hairpins. The ends were smooth against her fingers. She held them so that the sunlight fell on the diamond-crusted curve. "They're the color of your hair, Mother. Put them in so only the diamonds show."

"They're rather grand for daytime." Mrs. Reardon thrust the pins into the heavy coil of her brown hair. "But I'll wear them to please you."

"And Daddy. He gave them to you for Vincent, didn't he? Why would he give you a present and not Vincent? And when you give a present is it better to give what you like or what the person likes? Which is better?"

"It's better not to ask so many questions. Anyway, you can't always tell about presents. This house, now. It's a big house for the sake of this room. But my bedroom's where I like to sit and I never imagined such a pretty one."

"Tell about that," Veronica asked. "Tell about when you were a little girl and your house had a parlor and there were lace curtains in all the windows and the paper was all folded nice in the fireplace in case anyone would ever light it, only, of course, they didn't because Grandmother kept it just so."

"You seem to be telling me."

"Well, I only know part. I like better to hear about that house than when this was"—Veronica hesitated—"was new. And, anyway, I know about that." She went on quickly. "How you liked it better than a stable. Anyone would."

"What on earth?" her mother interrupted.

"Oh, I know, I heard Frank and Rita talking about it. They said you were glad Daddy got Pride's Tower, that he might have got a stable. But, of course, he wouldn't, would he? It was some kind of a stable, I can't remember, but, anyway, we couldn't have lived in a stable, could we? What kind of a stable was it?"

"A racing stable. And, thank the good Lord, he didn't. Though I don't know that this house is any cheaper. Now, shall I tell you about your grandmother's house, or will you wash your hands and have the red books?"

The red books were in the library. They were in Veronica's opinion the most beautiful books in the world. A forty-volume set of Shakespeare. The plays didn't matter to Veronica unless it was a good story like *The Tempest* or *Midsummer Night's Dream*. It was the pictures. There were beautiful colored pictures in every volume.

"I like the names, Mother, do you?" Veronica asked. "Say that hard one again, Helen something and who?"

"Helena and Hermia. You're like your father. He likes names. He might have picked all of yours from Shakespeare. As it was, you got the fanciest the calendar of saints had to offer."

"Read me the part where the queen goes to sleep."

Mrs. Reardon turned the page. "I shouldn't ever get cross at your father. Even in his foolishness he's lucky. He was bound to have every last thing in this house. And when I saw he'd bought even the books . . ." She looked at the tall shelves lined with blue and red and golden brown. "But there, the red books are worth it, aren't they?"

Veronica looked at the pictures. "Poor thing. Alone in the wood. And her boy has left her. But it ends all right. I guess she knows that. And that's why she looks so smooth and pretty in the pictures."

"We can't get to the end, Veronica. I'll take you up to Nanny."

At supper Veronica thought of the calm, lost girls in the wood near Athens. The lovely wood where you couldn't be really frightened.

"Want to play wolf again, Veronica?" Eugene asked suddenly. "I bet not. I just bet not."

"Oh, leave her alone," Jerome said. "She's too little for that kind of game. It's not her fault she got scared."

"I was not scared." Veronica remembered hiding in the friendly wood and pretending to be scared of the wolf. And then, gradually, the wood had ceased to be friendly and familiar. While Veronica crouched in silence, the wood had become a strange forest and she alone, hunted, afraid. She had run blindly and crouched, trembling, trying not to move. She hadn't been like Helena and her friend. She had forgotten it was a play.

"I was just pretending to be scared. For the game. I was just pretending, Jerome," Veronica said. And pretense had caught her suddenly. And the play was true and the wood was different and the branches moved threateningly and the small sound of a bird's wing, or of a twig snapping, was big with terror.

"That will do." Nanny pushed back her chair. "Veronica's too young for such games, as well you boys know, and I'll have no talk of wolves at my supper table. Now fold your napkins. And you've a bath to take, miss."

Veronica drew the thick cylinder of the rolled napkin through the silver ring. That was a good thing about being a girl. The boys just had plain napkin rings with their initials; she had a beautiful design. The curved lines made an *M* and a *V* and an *R*—Marie Veronica Reardon. It was hard to find the letters in the fancy pattern.

Veronica went to bed before the boys. She went to bed before everyone, except Vincent. Now Vincent was the baby. And that was good. Not to be the last, the least. Veronica had always been the baby except when there was Theresa. Veronica remembered only that there had been Theresa. When Vincent was born she had recognized the queer regular noise of his crying. And the red face and the thin little fingers that were so strong and sharp. Veronica had recognized Vincent because of Theresa, but she didn't remember Theresa. When Theresa was born, Veronica had been moved into the corner bedroom so that she hardly remembered sleeping in the big south bedroom. It seemed natural that it should be Vincent's room. Vincent was pretty now. Theresa had been pretty, too, in the end, Veronica thought, or had that been the flowers? She knew there had been lots of flowers. Had she seen them, or had she heard the others talking? When you were the youngest you listened a lot.

She lay still in the quiet room. She listened for footsteps that might pass on grown-up errands. And Vincent will listen to me. I'll tell him all about the other two babies who were born before Rita. Poor little babies. They are babies forever, but I am growing up. Now I am half as old as Jenny. Two times eight is sixteen. When I'm sixteen Vincent will be eight. And I'll do all the grown-up things and Vincent will only pretend. Poor Vincent.

Veronica wondered what Vincent would pretend. She would never know because he wouldn't tell. No one ever told. Perhaps no one else pretended. They did for games. But perhaps she was the only one who pretended when she was alone.

Veronica pulled the linen sheet over her face. It changed the last of the daylight into a cool whiteness. A light that belonged in no real time. A queer light. Like the light that shone when Princess Jacqueline drank the moon and read King Prigio's mind.

She would be invisible, Veronica decided. Tonight she would be invisible. She would have her ring of invisibility and walk through the house very quietly, very carefully, not to bump anyone. Rita and Bernardine and Jenny would be choosing their dresses and their matching slippers. Bernardine would have her big fan. She would choose the pale blue dress with the silver tassels hanging from the points of the skirt and the big blue feather fan. Blue for Bernardine and pink for Rita and white for Jenny. Veronica would follow them quietly down the stairs. And she would watch them in the red room with Frank and the other boys. Donald would be there and Jim Shea and a boy for Bernardine and they would play the victrola and dance a little, while they waited. They were always waiting for someone. And then the girls would pin the big pieces of tulle around their heads and they would go off. Veronica would watch them. She would stand very quietly between the heavy brocade curtain and the lace curtain. And the heavy curtain would make it dark so that she would see through the lace curtain. The front-door lamps would shine on the terrace, making wide yellow circles, and the headlights of the car would make a bright moving path under the trees, and then the lights would go down the drive and disappear around the curve and there would be just the sound of the motor and then that would be gone. And there would be only the front-door lamps and beyond them the end of the sunset on the right in the west, and in the east and all around the beginning of night. Veronica would wait very carefully until the front hall was empty so that no one should see the red curtains move. She would wait until her father and mother had gone into the dining room and the hall lights were dim and then she would walk quietly up the stairs. She would walk carefully in the pattern of the carpet and she would feel the thickness of the carpet against her bare feet.

The curtains would be drawn so that the stairway would be dark as it curved around the big chandelier, dimmed now with only a few of its lights shining through the blackness of the frame. And, suddenly, she would be afraid as she had been when she was little, when she had really gone downstairs after bedtime. All the grown-ups had gone out and the big chandelier had looked different, not as it did in the daytime, nor as it did when all its lights were blazing. And fear had come suddenly. Fear had come suddenly on the stairway, as it had come today in the wood when she had been hunted not by Eugene but by a wolf and the wood was a strange forest.

Veronica pushed back the sheet and sat up. She felt her heart pounding. It felt louder than the blue clock on the mantel. Her room was still bright with the sunset light. She climbed cautiously out of her high bed. She walked over to the mantel and stretched her neck to look at the beautiful fancy china clock. It was ticking nice and loud now between the elegant blue-and-white china lady and gentleman who stood at each end of the mantel. They had been her grandmother's best ornaments and her best clock. They had stood in the parlor. And then her mother had had them. And now in Pride's Tower they were hers. There was no room for them downstairs.

She moved to the embrasure of the west window. She was glad she lived on the third floor where the windows were deep in the slanting roof. She was glad that the sky was still bright above her mother's terrace and the garden and the fountain. The girls wouldn't even have started to dress. She was glad to be in the real brightness, not in the pretended darkness. Still it would be fun to have a ring of invisibility if you were careful with it. She used to believe you could have one if you wished hard enough. She used to believe that magic was there, right there, if you turned quickly enough. From old habit she turned but she knew that the blue-and-white pair were standing quietly. She knew, very well, that whether she watched them or not the china lady and gentleman never moved. That was because she was in the age of reason. Father Janvier had explained it. Seven was the age of reason. And Veronica was eight.

As she looked straight into the west the sky was bright. She pressed her nose against the screen and twisted her head, trying to look north where the edge of the dark must be. It was a beautiful sky but not so beautiful as the best sunset. The best sunset had been long ago when she was little. Four or five. That night the sky had been pink all over. Veronica had sat on the front steps and had waited for her father to come home. There had never been such a sky. There were pink shreds of clouds all over it. Veronica had watched and had grown a little dizzy as she held her head back to see all the sky. Then the motorcar had come around the curve of the drive and the headlights dimmed the brightness of the sky and turned the green to a queer color, an indoor green like a carpet, and the shadows of the trees were different and they moved too quickly. That was the night that her father brought the doll in the trunk from Paris. Veronica had named the French doll Genevieve after Jenny's real name. Genevieve had been part of the magic. She had everything. Not just dresses, but rice powder and a little bottle of perfume and a fan and jewelry pinned on a big piece of cardboard, a necklace of beads and a bracelet and a beautiful brooch. Veronica tried to remember the magic of the sky and the moving lights and the foreign doll. That was long ago when magic might be true. If you wished hard enough it might be true. It might all be true. You might find the ring of invisibility. And Genevieve of France might be more than just a doll from a toyshop, and the blue-and-white figures might be alive inside the china. You might see them move if you looked quickly enough. That was long ago before the age of reason.

Veronica jumped on her bed. She sat high on her pillow. She clasped her hands around her knees. This was better. It was better to understand. It was better to be into a time that stretched clearly behind you. The long time before hadn't been clear. She remembered only bits of it. She couldn't remember any of it right. Not even the night of the best sunset, not even the night when she had been frightened of the half-dark chandelier on the staircase. She knew she hadn't wanted its strange black world to come alive. Nanny had found her on the stairs. She had been afraid to run, afraid even to turn her head away quickly enough.

Veronica hugged her knees. This is better than the magic. Magic can be bad as well as good. It's better to be older than magic. It's better to understand. It's better to be well into the age of reason.

She smiled. Now I can't be mixed up any more. She rocked back and forth and sang a little song of triumph. I'll know more and more and more. I'll be like Rita and Bernardine and Jenny.

" 'Rule, Britannia! Britannia rules the waves!' " That's Nanny's song. " 'Britons never shall be—' "

The door opened. Nanny stood on the threshold. "What sort of a carry-on is this, I'd like to know?"

"I'm Britannia, Nanny. I'm Queen of England and Empress of India and—"

Nanny deftly removed the pillow. She placed Veronica flat beneath the covers. "Those boys! Getting you all excited at suppertime."

"It wasn't that, Nanny, it was—"

"Never mind what it was. This is no time for talking or for singing either. You just be quiet and go to sleep."

"But, Nanny . . ."

Nanny closed the door. It wouldn't have been any use telling

Nanny anyway. Nanny wouldn't understand about the age of reason. She was a non-Catholic like Lucy.

"Poor Nanny, poor Lucy," Veronica murmured.

All the Reardons were Catholics, and Jim Shea and Donald Moore. It was nice to be what everyone was. She turned her head and smiled at the ivory Madonna that stood on the table beside her bed. At the feet of the Virgin was a little gold case, no bigger than a locket. Veronica opened the case and took out her First Communion rosary. Her lips moved as a decade of the gold beads slipped through her fingers. "There. Now you can have them." Veronica draped the rosary around the ivory shoulders. A queen should have a necklace. *Holy Queen, Mother of Mercy.* Veronica wished she knew the litany, too. It had more beautiful words than the Salve Regina. She remembered Father Janvier saying them at Benediction in May. *Mystical Rose . . . Tower of Ivory, House of Gold . . .* She remembered the incense swinging on the end of the gold chain as Father Janvier moved. She turned her head on her pillow and looked at the figure, almost invisible now in the darkening room. This is better than the magic. *Hail, holy Queen, Mother of mercy; Our life, our sweetness and our hope, to thee do we cry, poor banished children of Eve; to thee . . .*

FROM *Uphill Walkers*

MADELINE BLAIS

LIKE ANY MOTHER, mine on occasion indulges an urge to cite the various ways in which she not only went to bat for us as children but also walked the extra mile and managed somehow to get water from stones as well as blood from turnips. She was widowed when I was five years: I've told that story often, left with five children, one more on the way, and ever dwindling resources.

In their marriage, my father got a premature berth at St. Patrick's Cemetery across from the Chicopee Moose Club.

He got the pickled adulation of a passel of children.

He got our prayers.

My mother got the house in Granby.

She got all the doctors' appointments, the calls from concerned teachers, the bills from various colleges. She got to take us to driver's ed.

She also got the challenge not to make his death her death too.

Being fierce, from New England, she took the words of the poet Robert Frost personally when he wrote, "Provide, provide." On the other hand, being Irish by heritage, she took Frost's meaning in the most unlikely light, not so much concerning herself with the homely task of supplying the basics in a cold climate, firewood and flannel, as dedicating herself to giving us what she thought our lives would have been like had our father, the true provider, lived: a swirl of lessons and opportunities and symbolic offerings, such as red meat and equestrian training at Mt. Holyoke College, back in the days when it operated a stable with lessons available to the public. Sometimes she cannot resist the urge to name all the ways in which she sought to enrich our lives.

Her most stunning entry in the good mother sweepstakes surprises her more and more with each passing year, the daring of it, the glamour, the sudden heedlessness of expense: She took us, one or two at a time, never the whole lot naturally, you'd need to be a saint for that, to New York City.

These excursions stood out. We were not the Grand Canyon type, not temperamentally suited to long car trips and lengthy pilgrimages leading to caverns with stalactites or empty battlefields or roadside stands that sold shells and tomahawks.

Mostly we just stayed put in the Bay State, which held its own amusements, such as maple syrup and melting snow. If my mother ever writes her autobiography, her chosen title is "Me, Maureen, from Massachusetts." Never a confident driver, she despised the Massachusetts Turnpike from the moment it opened in 1957 and spoke of it as if it embodied some deep evil, as if its soft shoulders were lined with thousands of dancing psych majors and myriad ladies clad only in sheets. In fact, I remember at times being so desperate for a change in scenery that when our mother used to get in the car simply to drive the mile or so to Dressels' Service Station for gasoline, we lay in wait for the telltale roar of the engine and then flew out of our rooms, propelling ourselves out the front door, diving into the two-toned blue Nash Rambler, which had the strange distinction of being both stodgy and salacious. Before we became teenagers the Rambler's most prized attribute, the way the front seats reclined to a horizontal plane, was lost on the Blais girls, the object of the same kind of snickering that attached to certain otherwise normal words, like *miscarriage* and *queer* and *balls*, when they were pronounced in a low, knowing way.

We didn't go to Boston, we didn't go to the Cape, we hardly went anywhere at all, but for reasons that had more to do with the kind of life my mother wished to live than with the life she was leading, she energized herself, with a remarkable fury, for her visits to New York City, which entailed a four-and-a-half-hour train ride and two nights in a hotel.

The routine did not vary.

First stop: Tall Gal's, which specialized in shoes for tall gals with narrow feet. She wanted something strappy and oddly hopeful that suited her quadruple A (or was it quintuple A?) heels. We ate at Horn & Hardart's Automat. The appearance of each sandwich in its metal compartment had the air of a certain kind of low-level miracle such as you might hear about in New Jersey or the Philippines: the Immaculate Conception of Cold Cuts. We visited the public library to admire the stone lions. We went to Lord & Taylor, where our mother sashayed into Better Dresses to inquire about the latest Anne Fogarty, rattling off the name of the designer with a kind of bored aplomb, the purpose of which was to establish once and for all that she knew Something about Something. Lunch followed, at the Birdcage Restaurant, which served sherbert and miniature sandwiches. (An unsolved mystery: what is it about the very word *sherbert* that always causes children to giggle and cavort?) On to more of the usual tourist hoopla, the Empire State Building, the Oyster Bar beneath Grand Central, Radio City, the Met to see the pictures of fat naked ladies and blurry landscapes, the Rainbow Room, for peanuts plus a view. I remember trooping behind my mother, while she sailed the streets, borne forward by a private breeze. The exhaust was a kind of perfume, the honking an aria, the jostling crowd an appreciative claque.

One time we took a sightseeing bus.

In the Bowery we saw the bums, as we called them, men warming their hands and their stubbly faces in the heat of barrels rosy with lighted trash. This scene served to launch my mother into her standard Great Depression reverie, a familiar spiel about how men she knew, proud men from proud families, were forced to leave their neighborhoods and go to places like Hartford, pronounced as if Hartford were the end of the world, and sell pencils and apples on street corners.

"You cannot understand how hard it was unless you lived through it," she would say, her voice trailing off, her gaze devouring the horizon. (Remembering now, I have an odd thought: "You don't understand." That could be my mother's epitaph.)

On that particular day in New York City, one of the men eyed the bus and assuring himself, falsely, that no one was watching, he took an empty bottle, smashed it on the pavement, and stowed it, shards and all, as future weaponry, inside his coat pocket. Later we went to Chinatown, where our mother got what looked like chopsticks to put in her hair.

She changed with each inhalation of pavement and commotion. The mother I was used to simply vanished. She was gone, the creature who loosened her bun and with the long, dark hair flowing over her shoulders would sometimes sit in a trance for hours on the sofa in the living room, the smoke from her cigarette competing with the smoke from the fieldstone fireplace.

In New York, trailed by one child or another, dressed in a suit, Maureen Shea Blais would transform, become a different, lighter person. Though well in her forties, she was pleased to realize she was making an impression, creating a tableau. When she returned home, she would sigh and say how much she missed it.

"In New York," she always said, "the men still whistle."

The Eldest Child

Maeve Brennan

Mrs. bagot had lived in the house for fifteen years, ever since her marriage. Her three children had been born there, in the upstairs front bedroom, and she was glad of that, because her first child, her son, was dead, and it comforted her to think that she was still familiar with what had been his one glimpse of earth—he had died at three days. At the time he died she said to herself that she would never get used to it, and what she meant by that was that as long as she lived she would never accept what had happened in the mechanical subdued way that the rest of them accepted it. They carried on, they talked and moved about her room as though when they tidied the baby away they had really tidied him away, and it seemed to her that more than anything else they expressed the hope that nothing more would be said about him. They behaved as though what had happened was finished, as though some ordinary event had taken place and come to an end in a natural way. There had not been an ordinary event, and it had not come to an end.

Lying in her bed, Mrs. Bagot thought her husband and the rest of them seemed very strange, or else, she thought fearfully, perhaps it was she herself who was strange, delirious, or even a bit unbalanced. If she was unbalanced she wasn't going to let them know about it—not even Martin, who kept looking at her with her frightened eyes and telling her she must try to rest. It might be better not to talk, yet she was very anxious to explain how she felt. Words did no good. Either they did not want to hear her, or they were not able to hear her. What she was trying to tell them seemed very simple to her. What had happened could not come to an end, that was all. It could not come to an end. Without a memory, how was the baby going to find his way? Mrs. Bagot would have liked to ask that question, but she wanted to express it properly, and she thought if she could just be left alone for a while she would be able to find the right words, so that she could make herself clearly understood—but they wouldn't leave her alone. They kept trying to rouse her, and yet when she spoke for any length of time they always silenced her by telling her it was God's will. She had accepted God's will all her life without argument, and she was not arguing now, but she knew that what had happened was not finished, and she was sure it was not God's will that she be left in this bewilderment. All she wanted was to say how she felt, but they mentioned God's will as though they were slamming a door between her and some territory that was forbidden to her. But only to her; everybody else knew all about it. She alone must lie quiet and silent under this semblance of ignorance that they wrapped about her like a shroud. They wanted her to be silent and not speak of this knowledge she had now, the knowledge that made her afraid. It was the same knowledge they all had, of course, but they did not want it spoken of. Everything about her seemed false, and Mrs. Bagot was tired of everything. She was tired of being told that she must do this for her own good and that she must do that for her own good, and it annoyed her when they said she was being brave—she was being what she had to be, she had no alternative. She felt very uncomfortable and out of place, and as though she had failed, but she did not know whether to push her failure away or comfort it, and in any case it seemed to have drifted out of reach.

She was not making sense. She could not get her thoughts sorted out. Something was drifting away—that was as far as she could go in her mind. No wonder she couldn't talk properly. What she wanted to say was really quite simple. Two things. First, there was the failure that had emptied and darkened her mind until nothing remained now but a black wash. Second, there was something that drifted and dwindled, always dwindling, until it was now no more than a small shape, very small, not to be identified except as something lost. Mrs. Bagot thought she was the only one who could still identify that shape, and she was afraid to take her eyes off it, because it became constantly smaller, showing as it diminished the new horizons it was reaching, although it drifted so gently it seemed not to move at all. Mrs. Bagot would never have dreamed her mind could stretch so far, or that her thoughts could follow so faithfully, or that she could watch so steadily, without tears or sleep.

The fierce demands that had been made on her body and on her attention were finished. She could have met all those demands, and more. She could have moved mountains. She had found that the more the child demanded of her, the more she had to give. Her strength came up in waves that had their source in a sea of calm and unconquerable devotion. The child's holy trust made her open her eyes, and she took stock of herself and found that everything was all right, and that she could meet what challenges arose and meet them well, and that she had nothing to apologize for—on the contrary, she had every reason to rejoice. Her days took on an orderliness that introduced her to a sense of ease and confidence she had never been told about. The house became a kingdom, significant, private, and safe. She smiled often, a smile of innocent importance.

Perhaps she had let herself get too proud. She had seen at once that the child was unique. She had been thankful, but perhaps not thankful enough. The first minute she had held him in her arms, immediately after he was born, she had seen his friendliness. He was fine. There was nothing in the world the matter with him. She had remarked to herself that his tiny face had a very humorous expression, as though he already knew exactly what was going on. And he was determined to live. He was full of fight. She had felt him fight toward life with all her strength, and then again, with all his strength. In a little while, he would have recognized her.

What she watched now made no demands on anyone. There was no impatience there, and no impatience in her, either. She lay on her side, and her hand beat gently on the pillow in obedience to words, an old tune, that had been sounding in her head for some time, and that she now began to listen to. It was an old song, very slow, a tenor voice from long ago and far away. She listened idly.

> *Oft in the stilly night,*
> *Ere slumber's chain hath bound me,*

Fond memory brings the light
Of other days around me.

Over and over and over again, the same words, the same kind, simple words. Mrs. Bagot thought she must have heard that song a hundred times or more.

> *Oft in the stilly night,*
> *Ere slumber's chain hath bound me,*
> *Fond memory brings the light*
> *Of other days around me.*
> *The smiles, the tears,*
> *Of boyhood's years,*
> *The words of love then spoken,*
> *The eyes that shone*
> *Now dimmed and gone,*
> *The cheerful hearts now broken.*

It was a very kind song. She had never noticed the words before, even though she knew them well. Loving words, loving eyes, loving hearts. The faraway voice she listened to was joined by others, as the first bird of dawn is joined by other birds, all telling the same story, telling it over and over again, because it is the only story they know.

There was the song, and then there was the small shape that drifted uncomplainingly from distant horizon to still more distant horizon. Mrs. Bagot closed her eyes. She felt herself being beckoned to a place where she could hide, for the time being.

For the past day or so, she had turned from everyone, even

from Martin. He no longer attempted to touch her. He had not even touched her hand since the evening he knelt down beside the bed and tried to put his arms around her. She struggled so fiercely against him that he had to let her go, and he stood up and stepped away from her. It really seemed she might injure herself, fighting against him, and that she would rather injure herself than lie quietly against him, even for a minute. He could not understand her. It was his loss as much as hers, but she behaved as though it had to do only with her. She pushed him away, and then when she was free of him she turned her face away from him and began crying in a way that pleaded for attention and consolation from someone, but not from him—that was plain. But before that, when she was pushing him away, he had seen her face, and the expression on it was of hatred. She might have been a wild animal, for all the control he had over her then, but if so she was a wild animal in a trap, because she was too weak to go very far. He pitied her, and the thought sped through his mind that if she could get up and run, or fly, he would let her go as far as she wished, and hope she would come back to him in her own time, when her anger and grief were spent. But he forgot that thought immediately in his panic at her distress, and he called down to the woman who had come in to help around the house, and asked her to come up at once. She had heard the noise and was on her way up anyway, and she was in the room almost as soon as he called—Mrs. Knox, a small, red-faced, gray-haired woman who enjoyed the illusion that life had nothing to teach her.

"Oh, I've been afraid of this all day," she said confidently, and she began to lift Mrs. Bagot up so that she could straighten the pillows and prop her up for her tea. But Mrs. Bagot struck out at the woman and began crying, "Oh, leave me alone, leave me alone. Why can't the two of you leave me alone." Then she wailed, "Oh, leave me alone," in a high strange voice, an artificial voice, and at that moment Mr. Bagot became convinced that she was acting, and that the best thing to do was walk off and leave her there, whether that was what she really wanted or not. Oh, but he loved her. He stared at her, and said to himself that it would have given him the greatest joy to see her lying there with the baby in her arms, but although that was true, the reverse was not true— to see her lying there as she was did not cause him terrible grief or anything like it. He felt ashamed and lonely and impatient, and he longed to say to her, "Delia, stop all this nonsense and let me talk to you." He wanted to appear masterful and kind and understanding, but she drowned him out with her wails, and he made up his mind she was acting, because if she was not acting, and if the grief she felt was real, then it was excessive grief, and perhaps incurable. She was getting stronger every day, the doctor had said so, and she had better learn to control herself or she would be a nervous wreck. And it wasn't a bit like her, to have no thought for him, or for what he might be suffering. It wasn't like her at all. She was always kind. He began to fear she would never be the same. He would have liked to kneel down beside the bed and talk to her in a very quiet voice, and make her understand that he knew what she was going through, and that he was going through much the same thing himself, and to ask her not to shut him away from her. But he felt afraid of her, and in any case Mrs. Knox was in the room. He was helpless. He was trying to think of something to say, not to walk out in silence, when Mrs. Knox came around the end of the bed and touched his arm familiarly, as though they were conspirators.

"The poor child is upset," she said. "We'll leave her by herself awhile, and then I'll bring her up something to eat. Now, you go along down. I have your own tea all ready."

Delia turned her head on the pillow and looked at him. "Martin," she said, "I am not angry with you."

He would have gone to her then, but Mrs. Knox spoke at once. "We know you're not angry, Mrs. Bagot," she said. "Now, you rest yourself, and I'll be back in a minute with your tray." She gave Martin a little push to start him out of the room, and since Delia was already turning her face away, he walked out and down the stairs.

There seemed to be no end to the damage—even the house looked bleak and the furniture looked poor and cheap. It was only a year since they had moved into the house, and it had all seemed lovely then. Only a year. He was beginning to fear that Delia had turned against him. He had visions of awful scenes and strains in the future, a miserable life. He wished they could go back to the beginning and start all over again, but the place where they had stood together, where they had been happy, was all trampled over and so spoiled that it seemed impossible ever to make it smooth again. And how could they even begin to make it smooth with this one memory, which they should have shared, standing like an enemy between them and making enemies out of them. He would not let himself think of the baby. He might never be able to forget the shape of the poor little defeated bundle he had carried out of the bedroom in his arms, and that he had cried over down here in the hall, but he was not going to let his mind dwell on it, not for one minute. He wanted Delia as she used to be. He wanted the girl who would never have struck out at him or spoken roughly to him. He was beginning to see there were things about her that he had never guessed at and that he did not want to know about. He thought, Better let her rest, and let this fit work itself out. Maybe tomorrow she'll be herself again. He had a fancy that when he next approached Delia it would be on tiptoe, going very quietly, hardly breathing, moving into her presence without a sound that might startle her, or surprise her, or even wake her up, so that he might find her again as she had been the first time he saw her, quiet, untroubled, hardly speaking, alone, altogether alone and all his.

Mrs. Bagot was telling the truth when she told Martin she was not angry with him. It irritated her that he thought all he had to do was put his arms around her and all her sorrow would go away, but she wasn't really angry with him. What it was—he held her so tightly that she was afraid she might lose sight of the baby, and the fear made her frantic. The baby must not drift out of sight, that was her only thought, and that is why she struck out at Martin and begged to be left alone. As he walked out of the room, she turned her face away so that he would not see the tears beginning to pour down her face again. Then she slept. When Martin came up to the room next time, she was asleep, and not, as he suspected, pretending to be asleep, but he was grateful for the pretense, if that is what it was, and he crept away, back downstairs to his book.

MRS. BAGOT SLEPT FOR a long time. When she woke up, the room was dark and the house was silent. Outside was silent too; she could hear nothing. This was the front bedroom, where she and Martin slept together, and she lay in their big bed. The room was made irregular by its windows—a bow window, and then, in the flat section of wall that faced the door, French windows. The

French windows were partly open, and the long white net curtains that covered them moved gently in a breeze Mrs. Bagot could not feel. She had washed all the curtains last week, and starched them, getting the room ready for the baby. In the dim light of the street lamp, she could see the dark roofline of the row of houses across the street, and beyond the houses a very soft blackness, the sky. She was much calmer than she had been, and she no longer feared that she would lose sight of the small shape that had drifted, she noticed, much farther away while she slept. He was traveling a long way, but she would watch him. She was his mother, and it was all she could do for him now. She could do it. She was weak, and the world was very shaky, but the light of other days shone steadily and showed the truth. She was no longer bewildered, and the next time Martin came to stand hopefully beside her bed she smiled at him and spoke to him in her ordinary voice.

FROM Manhattan, When I Was Young

MARY CANTWELL

I AWOKE ON MARCH 17, waiting. "They never come when they're supposed to," I told B., and sent him off to work. All day long I waited, dusting the furniture, scrubbing the bathtub, longing for the moment when, like somebody in the movies, I would bend over, clutch my stomach with both hands, and say—to whom? I was alone—"I think it's time." Meanwhile the baby was quiet, scarcely moving, hardly even stretching her legs. I know she could hear, but could she see? Do babies keep their eyes closed until they're born? Or do they open them, look around, study the terrain?

After supper, we went to the movies. With no baby yet in view, of course we would go to the movies. We saw *Our Man in Havana*, in Times Square, where Irish and Irish-for-a-day drunks were roistering down Broadway.

The next morning, on the dot of 8:30, I felt a dull ache in my back, which was repeated about fifteen minutes later.

"The baby's coming," I said, as cool and know-it-all as I had been the day before. "But it's going to take hours, so you just go off to work." My husband, obedient to the superb creature I had become, did as he was told.

So much to do! I had to go to the A & P so that B. would have something to eat for the next few days. Then I had to pick up the slipcovers I had left at the cleaner's so the living room would look nice. Waiting for the cleaner to find them, trying to distract myself from the contractions ("Don't sink pain!" Mrs. Bing was hissing into my ear. "Sink contraction!"), I studied the little plastic bird on the counter. It kept dipping its head, up, down, up, down, toward a glass of water. *I will never forget this bird*, I said to myself. *I will never forget this moment.*

"I'm in labor, I'm in labor," I wanted to shout to the people I passed on Seventh Avenue on the walk home. "Look at me, look at me, look at how it's done!"

On my hands and knees, I crawled around the couch and loveseat, closing the snaps that held the slipcovers to the tapes sewn to their undersides. Finished! I washed every dish, did a last run with the vacuum cleaner. Finished! I ate my favorite lunch, egg salad on white. Finished! And at last I crawled onto the chaise longue with Rose Macaulay's *The Towers of Trebizond*. I loved that book. Who wouldn't love a book that began " 'Take my camel, dear,' said my aunt Dot, as she climbed down from this animal on her return from High Mass"? But after a while I could no longer rise to Macaulay's High Anglican empyrean and dialed B. "Come home," I said, still calm, still grand.

Because we thought overnight cases tacky, bourgeois, my nightgowns and toothbrush were in a paper shopping bag, along with a handful of lollipops that were supposed to provide glucose when my energy flagged during labor. Together, with B. carrying the shopping bag, we walked out the door and up Perry Street to Seventh Avenue, and together we directed a cabdriver: "Doctors Hospital."

"Doctors Hospital?" the driver said. "I hear that's some place. Jackie Gleason was just there, and they tell me the parties were *something*."

Judy Garland dried out in Doctors Hospital, I believe, and it was a nice place to go after a suicide attempt and an even nicer place to go if you were having a baby, because it had room service. Queenly in my wheelchair, I watched while B. fumbled in his wallet for his Blue Cross card. Gracious even with an enema tube dangling from my backside, I chatted with the nurse while she shaved my pubic hair, faithful to my parents' creed that small talk could raise you above anything. Because I felt the pains—oh, no, the contractions—in my back, B. and my doctor did the *effleurage* for me, circling their hands over my spine while I lay on my left side, facing a bureau and focusing on a drawer pull. Only once was there a break in my Lamaze breathing. B. had ordered a sandwich, and the crunch of the pickle he was chewing distracted me. "Stop that pickle," I said. He stopped.

"Look," the doctor said, rolling me on my back and shining a bridge lamp between my parted knees. What pleasure to lie with my legs spread, pubis shaved, blood trickling, stomach swollen, an inch or so of dark head visible in my vagina, and nothing on a man's face but love and joy.

In the labor room, or so I understood, there were rails on the beds so the maniac maternals wouldn't fall to the floor. But here I was in a wooden four-poster, while a light snow drifted past the window. The window was slightly open, and through it I could hear the faraway whine of traffic fourteen floors down on East End Avenue. Sometimes the curtain rustled; sometimes there was a footfall in the corridor. There was no other sound beyond my "Huh, huh, huh, huuuuuuh." "The baby's crowning," the doctor said to B. "Help me wheel her to the delivery room."

Something happened next, a coincidence, which would be unacceptable in fiction and is barely acceptable in fact. But for one who believed then that the mills of the gods do indeed grind, it seemed reasonable, predictable even. On the way into the delivery room, we were stopped by a doctor who said to my obstetrician, "Do you want any help, Elliott?" He did not recognize me, but I did him. He was the doctor who had said I was too frail to carry a child and medicated me with a contraceptive. "No," I replied before my doctor could open his mouth, and we sailed on.

I had imagined bright lights and white-robed, white-masked nurses flanking the table, not a small, quiet room empty except for a nurse who was putting kidney-shaped bowls in a cabinet. No matter. I needed no encouragement, no towels dabbed on the forehead, only the doctor's "Push . . . stop . . . pant . . . push . . . stop." And at last, "Here's the head . . . I've got the shoulder . . . Mary, it's a girl."

"It's Katherine," I said, and let go of the handgrips.

Dying, even if the crossover is accomplished with a fanfare of bugles and the raising of a golden curtain, cannot be so profound a shock as the birth of a child. Nothing, not all the reading, not all the line drawings, not Mrs. Bing's big cardboard-mounted pictures of a baby traveling down the birth canal, had prepared me for the sight of a human being emerging from between my legs. Katherine had dark hair, two deep dimples, and was yelling.

The nurse, through finally with the kidney-shaped bowls, dried the baby with a towel, slid her into a diaper and a slightly tattered, too-big shirt, and said, "Ooh, look! She's got dimples."

"Will she keep them?"

The doctor, sitting between my knees with his head bent over a needle and thread—he was sewing up the episiotomy and looked like a tailor—laughed. So did the nurse, as she tried to hand me the baby.

"No," I said.

"Don't you want to hold her?" she asked, and again I said no.

"I might drop her."

They started laughing again but stopped abruptly, because I had started to shake. There was no controlling it; even my legs were trembling. The nurse gave up and took the baby away. I gave up, too, and closed my eyes while the doctor wheeled me back to my room and to B., who had just become a father.

"Shut the window," I said, trying to talk over what was happening to me. "Shut it. Don't let me get near it. Please, I want bed rails."

A carpenter came and nailed the window to the sill. *Ridiculous*, I thought as he hammered. *I can jump through the pane.* I heard the sound of breaking glass, felt myself hurtling with the baby in my arms, heard the splat when we hit the ground.

"Don't leave me alone. Get a nurse. Put me out."

A fat Irishwoman came and settled herself into the chair in the corner. Another doctor came in and injected something into my arm. The last thing I saw was the light and the hope fading from my husband's eyes, and the last thing I thought was that my baby, ejected now from the fortress that was myself, would never be safe again.

*   *   *

For years i could not think about, much less talk about, those weeks that followed my first child's birth. Now I can report, but I cannot interpret. Compulsion, depression, anxiety: I can work up a song and dance about them. Psychosis—there! I took the easy way out, I gave horror a name—is beyond analysis.

Dr. Franklin arrived the next morning. He came every morning after that and held my hand, and although I cannot remember what I said to him, I do remember that I said nothing to B., afraid that if I diverted one word from my psychiatrist I would weaken the lifeline that was slowly, and finally, beginning to connect me to him.

Besides, Dr. Franklin would not be horrified by what he was hearing, any more than he would have fainted while watching an operation. My husband, however, was not equipped to deal with sickness, or so I felt and so I still believe. If he could look into my head, I figured, he would run away. Still, my having excluded him from my madness must have seemed yet another way of excluding him from my life.

I begged my obstetrician to tie me to the bed. He would not. I begged him to move me to the psychiatric floor. He would not. How could I nurse the baby, he asked, if I were that far from the nursery? Strange. I, mad, knew what should be done. He, sane, would not do it.

One night the fat Irish nurse fell asleep in the chair and I, staring across the bed rails at her plump, pink, piggy face, panicked and woke her. "I saw on your admission form that you're a Catholic," she said. "Pray."

The hospital was full of wanderers, most of them diaper service salesmen popping up unexpectedly in one's doorway. But once a woman dispensing religious tracts slipped into my room and spilled badly printed exhortations all over my bed. She was trying to enlist me in Jehovah's Witnesses. Another time a nurse, young and pretty and so thin she scarcely left a shadow, slipped into my room and told me that nerves were the price one had to pay for being as delicately attuned, as sensitive, as we. Meanwhile the fat Irish nurse mumbled her Hail Marys and then, nodding off, as always, at midnight, left me to the devil.

When the nurse who worked the evening shift in the nursery, and who brushed Katherine's hair into different dos—sometimes parted down the side, sometimes down the center—brought her to me for a feeding, I would not let her leave, because the old Irishwoman ran off down the hall then to her cronies, leaving me free to crash the window with my beautiful, innocent baby in my arms. Early one morning, when the Irishwoman left to get my orange juice, I got out of bed and baptized my daughter with water from the lavatory faucet. At least she would go without original sin.

Friends came to visit. I smiled, I chatted, and if any of them wondered why there were rails on my bed, they never did so aloud. B. came every night, stopping first at the nursery to peer through the glass at his daughter, and told me who had called, who had written, what his parents had said, who had invited him for dinner. When my breasts swelled to blue-veined white globes—"You've got enough milk to feed every kid in the nursery," the night nurse crowed—he arrived, unasked, with nursing bras. "Size 40C," he said proudly, taking my abundance for his own.

"If you'll just let me out of here, away from this window," I said to my doctor, "I'll be all right." So he released me from the hospital a day early, and back I went to our basement apartment, frantic to feel nothing but Manhattan underfoot. But first we watched while the nurse dressed our child in the clothes B. had brought from home, gasping when she broke off the withered stub of the umbilical cord. Then she swaddled Katherine in the lacy knitted blanket and stuck the lucky booties on her feet and handed her to B., who smiled to see his baby, his lamb, in his arms.

JUST AS I HAD thought overnight cases bourgeois, so I thought a baby nurse a sinful self-indulgence. So I had asked our cleaning woman, Mamie, who claimed some acquaintance with infant care, to come in for a few hours every day for the week after I came home from the hospital. She came once, then never again, and when chided by a neighbor said cheerfully, "You know me, Miz Gibney. Can't handle responsibility."

For two days I sat alone, holding the baby until B. came home from work, afraid that if I put her down for more than a minute, she would stop breathing. I nursed her, too, although my nipples were cracked and bleeding, because I was afraid I would make mistakes with a formula. On the third day Hoppy, a practical nurse, arrived.

Hoppy was Jamaican, short and round and brown, and when she walked, her starched white uniform crackled and her spotless white shoes squeaked. She slung Katherine over her shoulder, rather like a dishrag, and commandeered the apartment, whistling or singing ("You've got to get them used to noise") as she moved from room to room. When Hoppy swaddled Katherine in a receiving blanket, it was because she "needs the comfort"; when she made me nurse the baby every time she cried, hungry or no, it was because she "needs the comfort"; when she asked Katherine, "Do they speak Latin where you come from?" I knew that like me, she believed in a room up in heaven where babies waited to be called to earth. When Hoppy was there, my daughter was safe, and until the night B. told me about Lewis, so was I.

Lewis, the first child of another editor and his wife, was four weeks old. "Kate's got a date for the junior prom," his father said when Katherine was born, and he sent her a split of champagne in his son's name. A few days before her birth, we had had dinner at their house and I had given Lewis his bottle, "for practice," his mother had said. Now he was dead, B. said, with tears in his eyes, and he had not wanted to tell me but had to for fear I might call Lewis's mother one bright morning and say, "How is Lewis? How are his burps?"

There were tears in my eyes, too, but Hoppy said, "No, no, Mrs. L., you'll spoil the baby's milk if you cry." So I didn't cry, and wondered if there had been something wrong in the way I had held the bottle.

That night, lying beside my daughter, whose bassinet I had put next to the bed so I could listen to her breathing, my right hand holding down my left so that I could not close them around the tiny neck and squeeze, I resolved that whenever I felt the urge to kill someone, I would redirect it and kill myself instead. The relief was tremendous.

Many nights I slept on the living room couch, leaving my husband alone in the bedroom with Kate. She was safe with him. Often I would stare at the tiny, pulsing fontanel, thinking of how easily my long strong thumb could crush it. Her neck was so little one hand could break it. I would not bathe her. My husband did. He thought I was afraid she would slip. I was afraid I would push. But every time

I felt my hands moving or realized that my eyes had been too long on her neck, her head, I determined again to harm myself before I could harm her. The decision to die is a great restorative.

After six weeks the sickness trailed away, dispersing in shreds, like clouds lifting. The fear of heights did not. Day after day Dr. Franklin stood me next to his twelfth-story window, put both his arms around me so I would feel secure, and said, "Tell me what you see."

"There's a man with a raincoat and a shopping bag, and I can see a woman pushing a baby carriage. There's a little girl crossing the street, and three cabs at the corner." Naming. I kept naming things, people, eventually emotions, and the naming gave order to chaos.

But the fear of heights—ah, the fear of heights. Even today I stay away from windows on high floors, and when circumstances push me onto terraces, I sidle along the walls, my fingers looking for crevices among the bricks. It never leaves me, that reminder that once upon a time I was crazy.

THE FIRST TIME I took Katherine on an outing, on a Sunday afternoon in May when she was six weeks old, the wheel came off her green plaid baby carriage. A garage mechanic repaired it—"On the house, lady," he said—and set me, grinning, back on West Tenth Street. There could have been no stronger line of demarcation between me and those people up on the Upper East Side, I thought, infatuated with my fecklessness, than the distance between a fabric carriage with dodgy wheels and a Silver Cross pram. Actually, B. might have preferred a Silver Cross pram, but it would not have gone with the new identity I was coining for myself: Village mother.

That day and many days thereafter I took my daughter to

Washington Square, to the southeast corner, where a big sycamore that I came to call the baby tree spread its branches over a large, grubby sandpit. A certain kind of Village mother spent hours there, offering chunks of raw potato to her teething child. The purest example (all struck me as variations on a type) was a sallow, stringy-haired young woman who, talking constantly, made much of her Jewishness and her husband's blackness. She brandished his color, in fact, as if it were a flag. Meanwhile the baby, scrawny and dun-skinned, was treated with the rough affection due a puppy. But then, rough affection—dumping one's offspring in its carriage, carrying it more or less upside down on one's hip—was, like the raw-potato teething tool, a function of Village style.

I would have loved to talk to someone, especially about Beech-Nut's as compared to Gerber's and whether pacifiers made for buck-teeth, but I was too shy to start a conversation, and nobody was inclined to start one with me, probably because my face is stony in re-pose, and forbidding. Still, it was pleasant under the baby tree—the drunks mostly clustered by the fountain, and the folksingers who pre-ceded the drug dealers hadn't yet arrived—and membership in the club to which I had so desperately wanted to belong was glorious.

About four o'clock, about the time the air began to turn blue, I would rise from the bench and kick up the carriage brake and off we would go, past the stern, beautiful houses that were all that was left of Catherine Sloper's Washington Square to Bleecker Street, where strolled another kind of Village mother. This one pushed an enormous perambulator in which lay, banked in pillows and laces and fleecy wools, a fat little boy who was almost always named Anthony. I know this because a silver tag on a chain, reminiscent of the kind that drapes decanters, invariably swagged his coverlet. There it was, inscribed for all to see: ANTHONY.

Lucky Anthony, to be going home to a crowd. Like a lot of people with small families and without a strong ethnic identity, I thought the spirits were higher and the sentiments warmer in big Italian and Jewish households. Not in B.'s Jewish household—he had never even had a bar mitzvah, and if his parents knew a word of Yiddish, I never heard it—but in the kind I had glimpsed in old photographs of tenement life. Snug as bugs in a rug those families were. I couldn't see the poverty for the coziness.

So when I saw Anthony after Anthony moving like Cleopatra on her barge through the dusk of late afternoon on Bleecker Street, I saw their grandparents and their aunts and uncles and cousins lined up to greet them. I saw first communions and weddings and funerals at Our Lady of Pompeii, and statues of saints dressed in dollar bills, and a network of Philomenas and Angelas and Roses stretched over the whole South Village. I envied Anthony all of them, for Katherine's sake. For my sake, too.

My mother, who was forever reminding me that she personally had scrubbed my every diaper and strained my every beet, was none-theless rich in household help—her mother and her sister and her widowed great-aunt—and when she had walked uptown with me, it had been "Good afternoon" and "Is she teething yet?" all the way. But these were strangers on the streets of Greenwich Village, and I, who had never lost my provincial chattiness, had only an infant to talk to. "Okay," I would say as I turned the carriage into Ottoma-nelli's meat market, "this is where we get the veal scaloppini for Daddy and me. And you, you're having cereal and banana."

Once I had wrestled the carriage into the areaway of 21 Perry Street, however, the miracle overtook me, the miracle that always overtook me when I unlocked the door to my own home. The stove, its pilot light like a votive candle, was waiting; the refrigerator was purring; the turn of a faucet would set a pot to filling. "Poor Butterfly, though your heart is breaking," I sang while I settled Katherine into her baby butler; "The most beautiful girl in the world," while I maneuvered her small silver spoon into her small stubborn mouth; "Bye Bye, Blackbird" as, one hand firm under her rubber-pantied rump, I waltzed her to her crib.

While I wished that my father had lived to see his grandchild, I no longer felt the curious pain—a strange, slow tearing-apart— that had crossed my chest whenever I thought of him. I gave up the hope, too, never quite lost, that someday he would walk into the room. And, blessedly, a recurring dream gave up on me: a dream in which I met him, in one of his Brooks Brothers suits and a felt fedora, walking down Fifth Avenue.

"Papa!" I said. "You're alive!"

"Yes, I am, Mary Lee, but you must never tell anyone or try to find me, because if you do, I will die." So I left him in the middle of a crowd on Fifth Avenue and woke up crying.

"But Mary," a friend said once, "your father *can't* have been flawless."

"He was till I was twenty," I replied.

Perhaps if he had lived just a little longer, it might have been long enough for me to have grown away from him. But he did not, so I am forever the daughter looking for the lap that disappeared. It is the same with Katherine. If I had not gone back to work, if I had been locked up with her until the morning she left for kindergarten, I might one day have seen her as distinct from me. But I did go back, before she could even talk, and so I retain an image of my baby and myself nestled into each other like a pair of *matryoshka* dolls. She is perfect; so am I.

FROM *The Mermaids Singing*

LISA CAREY

CLÍONA

I T'S THE RINGING of the telephone that wakes me. I've fallen asleep on the sofa—something I've been doing lately while Mary Louise watches the hotel on slow afternoons. Never before have I been the napping sort, but I suppose it comes with age.

It's Seamus ringing to say that he and Gráinne will be in on the four o'clock ferry. The girl's well enough to travel again. I'm happy, if a little nervous, that they will both be here for Christmas dinner tomorrow.

After I hang up the phone, my head still feels strange, ringing with the echoes of my dreams. I dreamed about my mother, scolding me when I was a wee girl. More of a memory really. I must have been just this side of seven years when I convinced my brother Colm to take me out in the curragh to gather seaweed for the fields. I plopped over the side after overextending myself to reach what I thought was a lovely-looking piece. Colm fished me out and when he brought me home soaking to Mum, she was livid.

"Ah told ye ne'er to go out in that boot!" she said, in the Northern accent she had which was so different from my own, and every other islander's. "Are ye wantin the mermaids to git ye?" At the mention of mermaids, I started crying. I'd heard enough stories of how heartless the creatures were, how they clamped onto you with their webbed hands and held you under, laughing bubbles as you choked for air. I tried to hold back my sobs; my mother hated it when her children cried. She spanked me that day, hard and unrelenting with my father's belt. My father never hit us, but she liked to use his belt for the appearance of authority, as on our island it was usual for the men to punish the children. Whenever she asked my father to unbuckle it, he did so slowly, as though he were the one about to be spanked.

I hated my mother that day—hated her most of the thirteen years I spent with her, that's true enough. Now I can look back and see that I'd frightened her, that the terror of me drowning had been hidden behind her rage. But at the time I only saw a mean, ugly woman who never smiled and hardly ever left the yard, for she hated to meet her island neighbors. My mother was never at home on Inis Murúch. Mind you, it's a lovely place, and I'll live here until the day I die and am buried in the graveyard up the road. But I'll admit that island people can be hard on strangers. My mother lived here for near-on twenty years and I don't think she had a friend besides my father. Islanders can spot it a mile away if a newcomer has any contempt for the place, and my mother had plenty. They won't forgive that.

I can still see every detail of my mother's funeral, as if it is happening right before me. She was laid out on the bed for the viewing. I myself had helped the island woman wash her yellow limbs and prepare the hair above a face gone stiff in that familiar displeased expression. All the islanders who had never welcomed her moaned pretend sympathy to my father.

"Ah, she was a good wife to you, Jared," they said. "It's hard-pressed you'd be to find a better woman." The urge to contradict and expose them boiled in my throat.

I had nursed my mother as she wasted away those last three months, the cancer spreading so quickly I don't think it left a bit of healthy flesh in her body. She had been mean until the end, and sometimes confused myself and my sister for the island women she despised.

"Say it to my face, you bitch!" my mother had growled at me one morning, before she'd lost her ability to speak. "I know well enough how you hate me. You'll be thrilled when I'm gone, so you can get your trampy hands on my husband."

"Mum," I said, backing away, the brush I'd been using on her hair held at a useless angle in front of me. "It's me, Mum. Clíona."

"I know who you are, girl," my mother said. Spittle ran down her chin like the foamy suds of washing-up liquid. "You're the daughter who wants me to die."

I cried then, begging her not to say such things, clinging to her with more affection than I ever had in my life. Because she was right, you see. I did want her to die.

At the funeral, Mrs. Keane came over to me to offer her sympathies.

"You'll miss her something awful, won't you girl?" she said.

"No," I said coldly. "I can't say I will."

Mrs. Keane was appalled. Of course, she was probably thinking even harsher things about Mum, but had the manners not to say so. "God help you, you're a vicious child," she said, turning away.

The whole island knew what I'd said before the day was through. I suppose that's how I got my reputation of being a hard woman, which still sticks in the old ones' minds today.

"Clíona O'Halloran will tell you straight," they say of me, though I can be as circumspect and hypocritical as the next person.

I was true as my word, sure. I didn't miss my mother, not for years. Not until my father died. I long for her now, with the pain of a child and the understanding of an old woman.

Brónach—the Irish word for sorrowful—was my mother's Christian name. It is only after my own life as a mother that I can see how the name suited her. If I could have just one moment back, one time when she was screaming at me in rage, then I could say: I'm sorry you're lonely, Mum. Maybe it would have made a difference; we might have wound up the best of friends, like Grace and Gráinne.

I wonder, sometimes, if Grace missed me when she was dying, if for the first time she saw me as I truly am.

I sometimes think God planned our lives all wrong. What's the use in learning the truth so long after the opportunity to use it has gone by? I suppose that's what the afterlife is for, though it's not so easy, even for a Catholic woman, to keep in mind the promise of resurrection when you're drowning in the deep sea of your own mistakes.

I stand on the quay and watch the ferry slide past Granuaile's castle, the tiny figures of Seamus and my granddaughter standing on deck, pointing and leaning toward one another so they can be heard over the roar of the engine. Seamus, though he's been half-way around the world, will always be an islander. I suppose it's the only thing Grace could never love about him.

When they climb off the boat, Seamus steps forward and gives me a hug, right there in front of Eamon and the other men on the dock. He lifts me a little off my feet, until I screech in protest.

"You're an awful man," I say, prying myself away, but he's laughing and I can't help but smile at him. He's happier than I've seen him in years.

Gráinne, poor girl, looks about half her age, pale and skeletal, her short curls standing up in the wind.

"I guess you're mad at me," she says, a gleam in her dark eyes.

"Ah, you're all right, girl," I say. "It would be nice if you told a person, before you went traipsing off to the city." I leave it at that. I don't blame her for going to look for Seamus, it seems the best thing really. I can see the affection they once had for each other is there still, just clouded a little by intervening years.

When we get to the hotel, Seamus leaves us alone, walking toward his own house. Gráinne and I sit in the conservatory, the last of the sun glinting off the glass behind her head.

Her hair has grown enough that it resembles the short, violet-black curls she had as a baby.

I hear one of the two hotel girls call out "Clíona," and Mary Louise's murmur silencing her.

"What does your name mean?" Gráinne asks, as I pour her a cup of tea.

"It comes from an old legend," I say. "Clíodhna eloped against her parents' wishes and sailed off in a curragh with her man. He left her by the shore of an island—some say this one—to go hunting, and a freak wave crashed in and dragged her under. He thought she'd drowned, but later the islanders said they'd seen her, and that she had become a fairy of the sea."

Gráinne is quiet for a moment, and I can hear Grace's contempt in my mind. "Figures," Grace once said, "you'd be named after a loser."

"She was probably better off," Gráinne says.

"Come again?" I say. I'm confused, not sure if she's referring to my daughter or my namesake.

"Well I'd rather be off with the mermaids then stuck with some guy who treated me like that," Gráinne says, sipping her tea, that look of fierceness in her eyes. Her features are Seamus's, but the expression is the image of her mother.

"It's just an old story," I say. "I think it's told to discourage girls from running away." I didn't mean to imply anything, but Gráinne's brow furrows viciously.

"I wasn't running away," she says. "I just wanted to talk to my father."

"I know," I say.

"But if I did want to leave," she adds, stiffening her bony shoulders, "I could. You can't keep me here. I know you tried to keep my mother here, but you just can't do that."

"I'd like you to stay, Gráinne," I say slowly, carefully. "Most island children leave when they're eighteen. Some come back, but the majority find something to keep them away. I made a mistake with your mother, Gráinne. I did not want to let her go. And I lost her—lost the both of you—because of it."

She cringes, the poor thing, when I say the word "lost."

"I hope one day you will feel at home here," I say. "But I won't force you, sure. I never meant to force you." She looks confused, like she expected a big row and my agreement has left her speechless. I'm a bit surprised myself. At how easy this feels.

"I guess I'll stay for a while," she says quietly, and I nod, passing her a scone—which she actually eats.

You're the strangest of the lot of us, I want to say to her. A bit of everyone and every place of our lives in you. I was an Irish woman lost in America; your mother was an American girl trapped on Inis Murúch. You, Gráinne, are a little of both, and have been dragged between the two like a hooked fish. You may never feel at home here, I want to say, or anywhere. But sure, you're the kind who can make a place for herself, wherever you are.

Gráinne is looking out the glass walls at the sun, which is setting like a pool of blood on the water. The gaze is not quite her mother's. Gráinne doesn't seem to be looking at what's beyond that sea, so much as she's looking at the water for its own sake. Sure, this could be just an old woman's wishful thinking.

All the words I long to say to her crowd and clot in my throat. I cough them aside and hope my eyes will speak for me.

"More tea?" I say, and she lifts her saucer with a shaky hand. I steady it with the spout and pour the red-brown liquid, steaming, over the lip of her cup.

FROM What Girls Learn

KARIN COOK

AT ONE O'CLOCK, I sat up, hungry, with sunspots in front of my eyes, and headed for the kitchen.

"Bring me something," Elizabeth said.

"Me too," Samantha called.

Inside, the floor felt cool against my bare feet. I wrapped a stack of sandwiches in a paper towel. I heard Mama's voice in the dining room. She was saying something about the tumor, about lymph nodes and chemotherapy. Why didn't she ever tell me the things that mattered? I lingered in the corner near the refrigerator, holding myself still. I could see all three of them hunched over catalogs and newsletters, spread out among them on the table.

"My sister had this one," Mrs. Teuffel said, tapping a picture with her finger. "You'd never know there was anything the matter."

Mama studied the page and raised one eyebrow. "I don't think so," she said.

"Why not?" Lainey said.

"I'm just not going to buy into the commercialization of cancer," Mama said, holding the catalog up in front of Mrs. Teuffel and Lainey. She sounded defensive, rehearsed. She cleared her throat and shrugged. "I'd just rather use one of those natural sea sponges I read about in some magazine."

Lainey and Mrs. Teuffel exchanged glances.

"Have you looked into a group?" Mrs. Teuffel said.

"A group?"

"For support," Mrs. Teuffel suggested. "No one can go through this alone."

"I'm not alone," Mama said. She arranged the magazines and pamphlets in front of her, pushing the stack back at them. "I have Nick. The girls."

I leaned my face against the smooth wall, happy to hear her say our names, relieved that she didn't feel alone. There was a long silence. Mrs. Teuffel chased a stray radish around her plate with her fork. Lainey folded open a catalog and set it in front of Mama.

"Frances, have you thought about a wig?" she asked gently.

"I guess I'll have to," Mama responded, "just in case."

I stepped away from the wall, straining to be sure I had heard correctly. My knees felt stiff from standing so still. My heart pounded loudly in my ears. Mama with a wig? It didn't make sense.

"Natural wigs are the best," Mrs. Teuffel offered, leaning over to look, "like this one from China. Really good wigs are made with Chinese hair."

Mama gasped. "Eight hundred dollars . . ."

"If you figure it in over a lifetime," Mrs. Teuffel said, "that is not a lot of money."

"That's right," Lainey said. "Think how much most women pay for a good haircut. If you paid thirty dollars, six times a year, you'd have it paid off in almost four years."

"Then what?"

"You'll have it forever."

"I'm not going to wear a wig for the rest of my life," Mama said.

"Of course not," Lainey said, soothingly, "but you could keep it styled and ready for emergencies."

Mama's face furrowed. She seemed to have a different idea about what constituted an emergency. She started to speak and then stopped, looked as if she was searching around for something else to do or say. My legs were numb, my left foot asleep. I cleared my throat and waited for Mama to notice me lurking in the hall.

"Hey, sweetie," she called, "what are you doing inside?"

"I'm hungry. Can I have a sandwich?"

"Of course," Mama said, pushing her chair out from the table and joining me in the kitchen. "Take some fruit, too."

She loaded my arms up with food and pressed me toward the door. I tried to get her to look at me, but her eyes were darting from the dining room to the countertop. I stepped onto the landing, the sun bright in my eyes, my skin stinging in the heat. Back at the blanket, Samantha was telling Elizabeth about how Jill Switt tanned her boyfriend's name onto her bikini line using vinyl stick-on letters.

"Cool," Elizabeth said.

"Not really," Samantha cautioned, "they broke up."

The bottoms of my feet were still cold from the kitchen floor. When I looked back at the house, I could see Mama's shape against the glare in the window; she was washing dishes, her head turned toward her guests, the flash of her blond hair bobbing in conversation. Maybe I'd made it up. Everything I'd heard, the whole conversation seemed of another life.

"Hey Tilden, toss me an apple," Nick called from the center of the lawn. He dropped the sprinkler by the maple tree and went out for a pass. I threw a small red apple at him, harder than I meant to, and hit him in the shoulder. He caught it in the crook of his arm and pretended to limp, clutching his upper body, as he walked over to the sprocket at the side of the house.

Samantha laughed and pulled apart an orange, passing around the slivers in even clumps of three. "He's kinda nice, isn't he?" she said, licking her arm from elbow to wrist to catch the juice.

With a sputter, then a hiss, the sprinkler rose up out of the lawn. Elizabeth and Samantha took off chasing the spray back and forth and leaping over the lowest part. Between sprints, Samantha adjusted her bathing suit, pulling it downward and snapping it under her bottom. Finally, Elizabeth stood still and let the spray hit her stomach, coming and going in both directions. They were laughing uncontrollably, their voices melding in the hot noon air. I covered my burned legs with a towel and sat as still as I could, imagining Mama in a long, black wig made of real Chinese hair.

THAT AFTERNOON, WHEN EVERYONE had gone, I walked in on Mama doing her exercises in the pantry. She was bent over, her right arm rotating in a wide circle, a box of dried plums in her hand.

"Just a little circumduction," she said casually. "How was your day?"

"Okay," I said.

She put down the box, picked up a can of Campbell's, and started over. I watched as she rotated her arm in the other direction. I studied her hair carefully—shiny with streaks of brown. It was looped under and clipped low at the back of her head with a wooden barrette. I stared at the pinkness of her part, trying to imagine her bare scalp.

"Are you going to lose your hair?" I blurted out finally.

"I might," she said. "But it's only temporary." Once again, she wouldn't look at me. She stopped and put the can on the shelf. "The Mosquitoes say we have enough hair cells to make many different heads of hair."

She took a deep breath, her eyes cast downward along the floorboard. She seemed a million miles away.

"Will you have to wear a wig?" I asked.

"Not yet, Tilden." Her voice was suddenly shaky. "But Mrs. Teuffel's going to take me to get one to match my real hair just in case."

I kicked the toe of my sneaker against the base of the wall, gently rocking the food on the shelves.

"Don't worry," Mama said, forcing a smile and catching my eye at last. "It'll be kind of like having a makeover."

I HADN'T HAD A haircut with a name since Dorothy Hamill. And there I was, the night before my sixth-grade graduation, about to get an Artichoke. From Elizabeth. I'd gotten the idea to go short from a news story I read about a group of guys in the Midwest who shaved their heads in a show of support for a teammate with leukemia. Given notice, Mama would never have allowed that kind of cut—had planned, herself, to keep her hair as long as she possibly could. She liked hers best when it was twisted up the back. If she'd used more bobby pins, it could have been a Lobster Tail.

Elizabeth didn't believe me when I first told her about the side effects of what the Mosquitoes were doing. I had to read out loud to her from the section under cancer and chemotherapy in *Our Bodies, Ourselves* as proof. Then, our pinkies linked in a promise, the way we'd have them when we were little, we made a pact to each cut the other's hair after dinner. We voted over a selection of photos and diagrams from *Seventeen* and *Young Miss* and settled on the Artichoke because the top could be styled to spike or curl. The caption under the drawing said, *For soft days and hard nights . . . the artichoke is the most versatile style around.* I agreed to go first.

Elizabeth propped the diagram up on an empty chair and set out her tools. With her eyes narrowed in concentration, she combed my wet hair over my face, down past my chin and cut around the top of my head, just above the eyebrows. Slick brown pieces fell onto my legs and covered the floor around me like twigs. She hummed as she worked to the tune of "Piano Man." Before long my hair was falling away from me in loose hunks. I could feel Elizabeth making mistakes, the sound of the scissors clanking fiercely, the blades cold against my head. It didn't look anything like an artichoke to me. Not even upside down. Not even when I fluffed my hair with my fingers to make the top pieces stand up straight.

Afterward, she bent to the floor. "You want it?" she asked,

gathering the longest pieces at one end and holding them out to me. "You could save it and make a braid."

I knew Elizabeth would back out even before she started to justify herself. It had gotten late, the scissors were wet and beginning to jam. I locked myself in the bathroom and refused to come out. I wet down my cowlick and singed my bangs with a curling iron trying to get them to feather. In the mirror my head looked small, my eyes huge and hollow. Nothing like this ever happened to Elizabeth.

After awhile, Mama knocked on the door. "Tilden, honey, come on out," she said. "Let's have a look."

"Never," I said.

"What about graduation?" Mama asked.

"I'm not going." I dunked my head under the running water and started over with the blow dryer.

"How short is it?" I heard Mama ask Elizabeth.

"Promise you won't be mad," she said.

"I won't."

"Promise."

"I promise," Mama said.

"It's pretty short," Elizabeth said, "like a boy's."

"Tilden, what will make you feel better?" Mama called.

I told her that the only thing that would make me open the door was if she forced Elizabeth to get an Artichoke too.

"Will you come out if I get one?" Mama asked.

WHEN I UNLOCKED THE door, Mama was waiting in the hall. "It looks pretty," she said, reaching out to comb what was left of my bangs over to one side with her fingernails. She sat me down on the lid of the toilet and moved my hair back and forth under her hands. She pulled at some pieces near my neck. "We'll just get Lainey to clean up these edges."

Then, she called Elizabeth into the bathroom. "I want to tell you girls something," Mama said, positioning herself between us and sitting on the edge of the tub. Elizabeth sat as far away as possible, on the counter near the sink, and kicked her heels against the cabinets.

"You're perfect the way you are," Mama continued, "don't ever change anything."

Mama said that focusing on beauty would distract us from what really mattered. It had always been her belief that beauty came in cycles. And that all women were beautiful in one of three ways: striking, classic, and inner. She said that to be strikingly beautiful meant that people would stop you on the street, do things for you that they might not otherwise do. "It is a beauty that elicits unusual responses," she said. "On the surface striking might seem like the best kind of beauty, but really, it prevents understanding."

Elizabeth gnawed at a hangnail, pulling it with her teeth until it bled.

"Don't you wish for striking beauty," Mama said, when she caught me staring at Elizabeth's blond mane. She looked me right in the eye. "It will prevent people from seeing you."

Classic beauty, on the other hand, was useful in that it told a great deal about a woman's life. It meant that her lineage was reflected in her face and that over time, after she'd worn it through experience, it became her own. I remembered that Grandma had said that. Mama had come from a long line of classic beauties. Women who received their rewards later in life.

Elizabeth gazed at herself in the mirror, then over at me, looking for the resemblance. At twelve, she had already developed a reputation as a beauty. The TransAlt guys acted surprised each time she passed, as if the wind had been knocked out of them. Her blue eyes were set in close to her nose and when she smiled, her full cotton-candy pink lips stretched to expose one tilted front tooth. When we pressed our cheeks close, it was easy to see that together we shared Mama's face. Apart, left to my own face, I felt separate, more a glint of Mama than actually part of her. I remembered overhearing Grandma say that Elizabeth had our father's features. I stared at her, trying to tease out the parts of her face that were different from mine, looking for clues about him. Imagining him, all light and laughter, with stronger bones and thicker lobes.

Mama took her hair down from the twist at the back of her head and bent it up to see what an Artichoke might look like on her. She smiled at her reflection and then at me. "I'm going to ask Lainey to cut my hair, too. That way we'll both have new looks when you start up at the junior high."

Elizabeth looked impatient. "Can I go now?" she asked, her fingers drumming at her sides.

"Sure," Mama said, dismissing her. Then, she turned to me and squeezed my arm. "Tilden, it isn't about hair, you know. The only beauty to strive for is inner beauty," she said. "That's what matters over the long haul."

LAINEY CAME BY AT the end of her TransAlt shift. It was nine o'clock, almost past our bedtime, and Elizabeth and I sat silently watching as Lainey quartered Mama's ponytail with rubber bands and began sawing the hair just above the top band with the scissors. Little pieces sprang free. Mama pulled and measured each strand against her chin. I watched her face for disappointment. But she smiled the way she always did in the world, making it hard to know what she thought. At the end, Lainey was left holding a solid rope of Mama's hair, like a tail. She dropped it in a plastic bag and set it aside. She glanced at the photo of the Artichoke in the magazine and went on to give Mama some layers, talking through each step. When she held up the mirror, Mama dipped her chin to each side.

"You have a wonderful line," Lainey said. "You could even go shorter."

Mama blew her hair out with the dryer, fuller at the top and longer at her neck.

"She looks like Mrs. Brady from TV," Elizabeth whispered to me.

"No, she doesn't," I said. "It's shorter." To me, she looked the way the model in the magazine had looked, just the way I'd wanted my hair to look—perfect layers with a wave in back. Nothing ever came out right on me.

Lainey trimmed the jagged edges of my hair and painted my fingernails while Elizabeth sulked in the corner. It was almost eleven o'clock when Lainey left and Nick came upstairs to investigate. He appeared apologetic as if he was intruding. I watched his expression, waiting to find surprise in his face. Instead, he smiled big at Mama and kissed her hard on the neck.

"I feel like I'm living with two Twiggys," he said over her shoulder.

I gave him a blank stare.

"That's a compliment," he said.

As we were cleaning up, sweeping stray hair into a prickly pile, Elizabeth picked Mama's rope of hair out of the bag and held it up to her nose, inhaling the smell of it deeply.

"Put that back," Mama said. Her tone was a shock: harsh and punishing, it made Elizabeth cry. Mama moved to comfort her. "I just don't want it floating around," she added softly.

THE NEXT MORNING, I overslept and by the time I arrived at Brooklawn Elementary, the entire sixth grade was lined up in the hall, ready to march. Samantha leaned out of her place in line, showing off her sandals with wedge heels. Her hair was braided down her back with sprigs of baby's breath at the top and bottom.

"You look *so* different," she called to me.

The graduation march came over the loudspeaker in the gym and just as we had rehearsed, the whole line swayed forward to the beat. As we walked slowly across the waxed gym floor, I felt a sadness rise in me. This hadn't even been my school for very long and already it was time to leave. There were schools in Atlanta I had been at longer and had no certificates from. I didn't understand what the big deal was about the sixth grade. I looked at the bleachers to see if I could find Mama, but only the top of her head was visible over the crowd. Nick stood at the side taking pictures of kids who weren't even my friends. The slow, hollow sound of the music made my throat tighten. When Mr. McKinney called my name, I felt hot and flushed. Ms. Zimmerman squeezed my hand for a long time before giving me my scrolled certificate. Her touch almost made me cry.

That afternoon, Elizabeth and I made up, silently, while Mama and Nick were out getting a cake. Mama's room was still, the light making window panes on the carpet. I found Elizabeth up to her elbows in the large mahogany dresser by the bed. We moved wordlessly through Mama's things—holding up scarves, leg warmers, wooden beads—and draping each other in her favorites. At her closet, we pushed through the hangers, coming by her fancy clothes: a denim dress, maroon suit, and beige Angora sweater. Elizabeth smiled. These were the clothes Mama wore when she had something official to do involving the school or any occasion when pictures might be taken. We slid pieces of these clothes on over our own and moved around the room like grown women.

It was Elizabeth who found the wig, hidden at the back of the closet, tucked away behind Mama's shoe boxes and shrouded in tissue paper. She put her hand out as if to touch a shy dog and brought it into the light. Neither of us said a word. Similar in style to my own hair, round with stiff dirty blond hair, the wig looked more like an overgrown cabbage than an artichoke. Elizabeth folded her thick, blond hair up and tucked in the stray pieces with her free hand. From an angle, in the mirror, she looked almost exactly like me. For a moment, I was filled with pride. Myself, but better. It wasn't the right feeling, I knew. Looking at her, I imagined for the first time what it would really feel like to be beautiful. Elizabeth turned from side to side in front of the mirror, making pouty, sexy faces, watching herself from all angles.

There was no way to know just then all that was to come: that the neighbors would bring Mama an entire assortment of headgear—a bag of patchwork bonnets and terry cloth turbans left over from their friends who had battled cancer; that rather than order a wig made of natural hair, Mama would choose to wear this synthetic one into a nubby cap. It was impossible to imagine, standing there, that this wig would become part of her; that a year into the treatments, she would be casual with it, like a best sweater, tossing it on a chair at night, fluffing it out in the morning.

That day, all that mattered was putting everything back in its place, closing drawers and closets, desperate for things to appear as they had before. At the door to the hall, we stripped down to our panties and left our own clothes in a heap. We raced each other down the safe tunnel to our bathroom where we climbed in the tub together. While Elizabeth worked the faucet, I poured in the shampoo and waited, bent in half, for it to bubble up over my thighs. As the steam fogged the mirrors and the water rose around us, puckering our fingertips and the pads of our toes, we forgot about what was happening to Mama, forgot our worst fears, even forgot our fights. We stayed this way a long time, waiting for Mama to climb the stairs and find us, wrinkled and pink, rinsing our heads under the faucet. We were too big really for a shared bath, our knees knocking against each other, careful in the placement of our feet.

My Mother and Politics

MARY DOYLE CURRAN

My mother was a wild Democrat, my father a rigid Republican. Our dinners were one long argument. Very early I was introduced to the political scene.

I woke one morning to hear my father grumbling about the polls, a word that was entirely mysterious to me. My mother, up earlier than usual, was sitting on the side of the bed undoing her braids. She answered my father's grumbling with "Oh, go scratch." I knew something was up because she put on her best dress, a blue silk. She dressed very carefully and said, "Well, I'm off to the polls." My father turned his back on her.

It wasn't long, however, before the words "polls" and "politics" were very familiar to me. I couldn't have been more than six when my mother, who was head-checker at the polls, had my brother and me stationed outside the polling place, distributing flyers. She was very canny. She knew that the policeman would allow kids close to the entrance to the polls, although it was illegal. I can remember standing out in front of those places, rain or snow, passing out pieces of paper with strange men's faces on them. People would pat me on the head according to their political affiliations. I'd go into the crowded basement to get more flyers from my mother. She'd be sitting at a long table with a long list of names before her. She politicked even at the polls with "Good morning, Mrs. Cassidy. How's your John? Has he a job yet? You know our man is for the unemployed."

When I was just slightly older, I attended committee meetings and rallies. Most of the time the committee meetings were held at our house because my mother was chairman of the Democratic party in Ward Seven. My father would retreat in disgust to John McHarp's pub. The doorbell rang constantly as both men and women crowded into our parlor. The room would fill with cigar smoke. There was a roar of conversation. I'd retreat to the corner with my dolls while my mother argued, cajoled and ordered people around.

My mother had the perfect strategy for getting votes: the most-liked woman on a street, the woman with the most relatives. She chose women to do the doorbell ringing and to deliver the relatives' votes because, she said, "A man is off to a pub or the committee room where there's warmth and beer. Women will stick to their jobs without any temptation." There was no beer at committee meetings at our house, and when the cigar smoke got too dense, my mother would open a window and order the men to throw their cigars out. The men would do so, complaining about the lack of a good shot and the loss of their cigars. But no one disobeyed because my mother was the best organizer and best vote getter in the precinct. It wasn't that she was against drinking. My father always brought her back two bottles of Porter every Saturday night. I could hear the bottles being rolled under the bed when she finished them. But there was no drinking at her committee meetings because, she said, "Anyone who comes for the booze is not a serious vote getter."

I watched her one evening. She had a map of every street in the precinct before her. She pointed her finger at a street and said, "That's Mary Sullivan's street." Turning to Mary Sullivan, a fat jolly woman with seventeen children, she said, "Who can you deliver?" Every house on the street was marked with the name of an occupant or occupants. Mary Sullivan, standing beside my mother, said, "Well, I sat with the Delaneys' child while she was sick. They're for us, and George Meaney got his job through my husband going to the Mayor. He'll be for us. Then there's the Clearys—I helped wash their dead mother, and I know she was for us, God rest her soul, but I'm not sure of him. Maybe if we offered him fifteen dollars to be a poll watcher, he'd be for us. God knows he needs the money badly." Every house was marked with a star if the vote was sure. Others were marked with a question, and my mother did this very carefully. Then she said to Mary Sullivan, "The questions are the ones to work on. Never mind the Robinsons, they're strict Protestants. But you can get the Kellys' grandmother's vote. Tell them we'll send a car for her."

My mother's greatest defeat was the Old Woman's Home on Pearl Street. She even went and canvassed herself, dragging me by the hand. I was required to sing for the old ladies who stared at me blankly, clapped politely and went to the polls and voted Republican.

I didn't mind the rallies. They were fun—the halls all decorated with posters of the candidates—red, white and blue bunting surrounding them. There was always some Irish tenor who started the evening off with "The Star-Spangled Banner," and there was always a priest who ended the rally with a prayer. In between, there were endless political speeches, but also there were paper hats and popcorn.

I rarely listened to the speeches except when Mayor Curley from Boston spoke. He had a voice like a silver-tongued flute. It rose and fell rhythmically. I found myself carried away by the sound, paying no attention to the rhetoric. My mother adored him, and her proudest moment came when he shook her by the hand and said, "Mary O'Leary, a gem of a Democrat. And this is your little girl. I understand she's a true Democrat, too," and he patted me fondly on the head.

Mayor Curley was her idol, and she could always get money for her precinct from him. "You see," she'd say when someone attacked him as a crook, "he may be a crook (which she didn't believe), but he has his hand out to you and he passes it around. Let no one make a mistake. He's for the poor man." She liked Honey Fitz, too, but I preferred Mayor Curley's delivery. The rallies were like religious devotions, but they were noisy—everyone worked up to a pitch by the oratory. I heard the shouting and clapping in my dreams all night.

But it was best of all if our candidate won. The extras would be out in the street about ten o'clock. We all sat in the living room, waiting for the boy's shout of "Extra, extra." My mother would rush down for one and the words SULLIVAN WINS would be spelled out in huge black headlines. There were no Hiroshimas in those days, so they saved the big print for elections. Then off we would all go to Headquarters and the torchlight parade would begin. Hundreds of people carrying torches wound through the streets, usually ending up at the candidate's house where he would appear to be cheered and cheered. Then the parade would walk back to Headquarters for the acceptance speech and free drinks. The party would go on and on. My mother usually found me curled up in some corner asleep. We'd be driven home about three in the morning to my furious father who'd shout, "You're ruining that child's health." My mother's invariable answer was, "Well, it's her soul I'm after."

And this was true. Politics for my mother was a religion, closely connected with her own faith. But when the first Catholic President, John F. Kennedy, was elected, she said, "They'll crucify him."

The most exciting election I remember in connection with my mother was the first Roosevelt election. There were constant fights at the dinner table. My father was staunchly for Hoover because Hoover was going to maintain a high tariff and not undercut the American working man—this, despite the fact that my father had been out of work for two years. "Besides," he'd shout, "that Roosevelt is no better than a Communist." I've never seen my mother work harder for any candidate. She was going night and day, and the blanket of gloom that had spread over our house because of poverty seemed to vanish. She was gay and tireless, and she laughed away my father's tirades with, "For the working man is it? Well, may you starve under him."

The rallies were even wilder, the campaigning more intense. My mother was murderous against Hoover. "A chicken in every pot. There's only his own pot filled with chicken these days." Every time Roosevelt spoke, she read reports of it carefully. She even went as far as Boston to shake his hand. When Roosevelt was elected, she went wild. My father sat in his chair, gloomily predicting doom. She was so elated that she even allowed me to be in a church minstrel show, where I sang with a full heart and an empty stomach—"Happy Days Are Here Again."

Her interest in politics has never abated, and she is almost always uncannily right. During the Eisenhower administration, when the trouble at Little Rock broke out, my mother wrote me "that P Eisenhower better get down to L Rock and quit playing golf." She always knows what's going on, but she learns it from newspapers, not from television which she hates. When the first astronauts went up, she announced firmly, "I will not go to the moon." She prays devoutly for Roosevelt, John and Bobby, and her name for Nixon is "Tricky Dicky."

She made me into a political animal. All my boundaries expanded. I moved rapidly from Seven Thorpe Avenue and Hampden Street to the city, the country, the world, but not to the universe.

Mother and "Miss E."

M.F.K. Fisher

EDITH, MY MOTHER, really understood dried-up hometown librarians better than anyone I know. She had a pet one always on hand when we were in Whittier and was in cahoots with her about things like my bringing home eight books once, when I was perhaps six, from the children's basement in the public library. The young (but already dried-up) librarian, of course, called Mother and told her that I had lied through my teeth, since I knew that only two books were allowed to be taken out at night by children. Mother was properly chilly and embarrassed.

Then the young dried-up librarian said she wondered how old Mrs. Holbrook was getting along. My mother replied that her mother was doing very well indeed and had not been ill for some thirty years, and then it came out that I had told the librarian my poor old Irish grandmother was on her deathbed and that she needed me to read to her ... all night long, every night. Of course, this blatant fantasy was nipped in the bud, and from then on I was allowed to take only four books out at night, instead of the usual two.

As I look back on it, the episode proved Edith's power over the whole system, and I am glad that I was to benefit from it all my life, or at least until after she died. It was then that I realized *why* (and *when* and *how*) Mother had always been, in her bizarre treatment of dried-up librarians. I learned at last that Miss E., who for some twenty years had been the object of our extreme disaffection as well as mockery, had loved Mother dearly and loyally. This was partly because once a year, at Christmas, Edith always sent her a flamboyantly sexy and extravagant nightgown.

Of course, as we matured, we knew of these strange gifts, and Mother herself even discussed them and now and then showed us her yearly purchases with what was almost a titter from her and a universal snicker from us, her children. She'd spread out the beautiful gauzy flimsy whimsies over her bed, and we would make cruel, stupid, and often funny remarks about them, and about the person whose skinny old body they would soon hang on.

Of course, we envied Miss E., or her temporary equivalents, for we were young and spoiled and at times even given to moments of beauty, and Mother never bothered to shower us, her offspring, with any such extravagant dainties. This was a yearly custom, one of many in our household, but one we all puzzled over with obviously latent jealousy. We were convinced that Miss E. never really knew what to do with these exotic offerings.

Then, after Edith died, the dried-up librarian wrote to me from her desert "retirement home" such loving and even adoring letters as I hoped never to see again. They were amazing to me, and I knew that Edith had been right and that she had not bought the servitude of the strange remote disagreeable "old maids" for all those years in Whittier but that she had instead understood and appreciated something that was beyond our own caring or understanding.

To us, the children, Miss E. was a kind of ridiculous public dictator of our tastes and needs. We hated her for refusing ever to give us anything from the Closed Shelves, even when Mother would telephone to request that these sacrosanct supplies of local pornography and filth be opened to us. Miss E. stayed adamant, even in the face of Mother's yearly Christmas sensuality; she refused to heed the doctors, the local priests, and the pastors when they suggested that some troubled soul might find in her library a book that would instruct them better than their professional ethics could.

Once, when I came home from boarding school in a real puzzlement about the lesbian pleasures that were suddenly too much for me to understand and Mother asked Miss E. to let me take some books from the Closed Shelves, there was a firm *no!* Briberies, Christmas or otherwise, apparently meant nothing to this strange arbiter of our local morals. Mother ordered copies of most of Freud, Jung, Adler, and Krafft-Ebing, carefully and through "our" doctor Horace Wilson, and after she and I read them, she presented them to the library, as she had almost all the other good-dirty-sad books that were on the Closed Shelves there.

I remember that while we were waiting for the currently undesirable psychological exposés to arrive, Mother saw to it that I read *The Well of Loneliness* by Radclyffe Hall before she presented it to the Closed Shelves. Miss E. never acknowledged the presence

of any of these books, just as she never thanked Mother with anything but a short impersonal note at Christmastime for her sexy
nightwear.

Edith was Miss E.'s despair in many ways. She asked for and
got any book that she did not care to invest in herself, and her
deplorable taste in detective stories was locally known by anyone
who visited the library, since Miss E. religiously let her read them
first, before they went on the public shelves. Thanks to Mother's
cryptic and avid habits, we had complete runs of every English
writer of mysteries, from Agatha Christie on up and down, and our
collections of Dorothy Sayers and her ilk were the best and the
newest always, in California or even in America. Of course, our
own shelves were always full of new books as well as old ones, but
Mother was not about to invest in everyday literature when Miss
E. was so amenable to her suggestions, and I feel sure that the
Whittier Public Library circulated more current British and even
American fiction than any other small Carnegie in the country.

Of course, Mother loved anything *English*, but her taste was
good. We read *The Forsyte Saga*, but we also knew all about Vanessa
Bell and the Bloomsbury gang almost as soon as they did themselves, and Leonard Woolf and his wife were as familiar to us as
were the Churchills and even their American counterparts, the
Roosevelts of both Republican and Democratic leanings. The Ho-
garth Press worked hard to provide us with Anglophilic trash as
well as the "good" stuff. We read *The Spectator*, along with *The
Times* and the lesser London kitsch, and all the American period-
icals that were then in the mails.

This last important part of our literary upbringing was due less
to Edith than to my father Rex, who subscribed to every periodical

in print in America, whether or not it was free to him. He himself read probably ten magazines a week, and we all had a running undeclared war with him about remembering the plots of each continued story in every one of them. We prided ourselves on never reading the weekly résumés, and it was a game that was played with great success for more years than I can now remember. Father, of course, read the magazines first, but as soon as he laid down an issue, it would be snatched up by one of us children and read as fast as possible.

Collier's and *The Saturday Evening Post* had perhaps the best serials, but there were also real dillies in magazines like *The Ladies' Home Journal* and *The Woman's Home Companion* and *Redbook* and *Cosmopolitan*. And then of course there was *The American Boy*. And Grandmother Holbrook saw to it that we always got—and *read*—*The Youth's Companion.*

And then there were all the magazines like *Motion Picture*, and there was something about automobiles always, and there were several farm journals and then house organs of clubs and organizations: Elks, 4-H'ers, and later Rotarians and Lions and the Kiwanis Club, and *The Iowa Morticians' Quarterly*. And then there were the literary digests—*The Atlantic Monthly* and *Scribner's*, wonderful things by Aldous Huxley about LSD or mescal buttons, and a long story by Scott Fitzgerald once, and always Upton Sinclair somewhere around—and Bernarr Macfadden's several different monthlies, all about diet and physical culture and how to conceive boy babies instead of girls, and so on. And there was *The Masses*, which I read hungrily when I was thirteen or so.

And all the time, as a kind of background to Mother's Anglomania and Father's Chicago-to-Whittier newspaper life, there were the reminders of Miss E.'s disapproval of our concerted and wild-eyed literary spree, which continued uninterrupted from about my fourth year in Whittier to the final bulldozing of the Ranch house when I was nearing fifty. By now I think of Miss E. as a sort of goddess, unwitting certainly and willy-nilly, floating austerely above our unconscious heads, wearing a very sexy nightgown over her presumably chaste body. She's rather like the airborne fellow who plays the fiddle in many of Marc Chagall's pictures: omnipresent and unexplained. She's much clearer now than when she was trying so desperately to curb our hungers and to keep them under proper local control.

In actuality, she was a tall, thin woman with faded colorless hair and skin, and she dressed properly in clothes that would fit her position as head librarian, which is to say in a way that made her almost invisible. At least, that is how I remember her in the name of my grandmother and my parents and my siblings. But by now, and in my mind anyway, and from her letters to me when my mother died, she has turned into a really loving woman, gracious and adoring, dressed always in those sheer, alluring, glamorous, and completely unfitting nightgowns that my mother gave her for so many years, in spite of our derisive mockery. And I wonder who actually got the most pleasure from them. Certainly my mother did not need to buy her way through the Closed Shelves, any more than Miss E. needed to be so unfailingly severe and disapproving.

ELIZABETH GURLEY FLYNN

THE NAME "GURLEY"

MY MOTHER, ANNIE GURLEY, landed in Boston in 1877, at the age of seventeen. She was very beautiful, with blue-black hair, deep blue eyes, a soft white skin and regular features. She had a clear and cameo-like profile. She came from Galway on the west coast of Ireland, where it is reported the people have "Spanish blood," flowing from the shipwrecked sailors of the defeated Spanish Armada, who settled there in the sixteenth century. To this is attributed our black hair. The first of the Gurleys, her aunt Bina and later her uncles James and Mike, had come to Concord, New Hampshire, before the Civil War, in the migration which took a million men and women, from 1847 to 1861, away from Irish famine and political persecution. My mother was the oldest girl of thirteen children, but she was brought up away from home by her

Gurley grandparents and spoke only Gaelic in her childhood. She had a faint trace of it in her speech.

Her childhood in Loughrea was a happy one. The Gurleys in Galway, where they say, "God bless us!" were much more prosperous than the Flynns in Mayo, where they say, "God help us!" She lived on a farm, where there were all sorts of domestic animals. She was taught at home by her uncles, because they boycotted the National (British) schools. Her grandmother, kind to all others, would give nothing to a "uniform." She refused food, milk, or even water to British soldiers, who had to go seven miles further to town for supplies. When the Irish labor leader, James Larkin once criticized American women for smoking, my mother said smilingly: "Well, Jim, I used to light my grandmother's pipe with a live coal from the hearth!" When another Irish friend turned up his nose at "the garlic-eating Italians," she told him that her grandmother used to pull up garlic in her garden like radishes and eat it raw. She had a theory that the Irish were "the lost tribes of Israel" and told us how her grandfather killed animals for food in the same manner as the Jewish people, and that Saturday began the Sabbath and all work closed on his farm. Mama did not deny the faults or glorify the virtues of the Irish, as our father did. We were amused at this and often said, "Papa is more Irish than Mama and he never saw Ireland!"

The Gurleys were Presbyterian, but not very devout. My mother knew all about fairies and leprechauns and "the little people" who are supposed to inhabit Ireland. She was not brought up religious and did not go to church, however. When we asked about this, she would put us off whimsically by saying: "After all, the Irish are pagans at heart!" She had a few pleasant years here with her relatives in Concord, until her father died in Ireland and her mother hastily sold the good land he had owned and cultivated and brought her brood of nine children to America. They were all in their 'teens. She left seven here and returned to Ireland with the two youngest, whom she placed in an expensive convent school. My mother was forced to become the head of a new household, to support and bring up her brothers and sisters. To do this she worked as a tailoress on men's custom-made coats, for thirteen years. She did exquisite hand sewing, especially on pockets and buttonholes. She helped all her brothers to learn trades—Jim and Martin became plumbers, John a leather worker, and Mike a metal worker. All were members of the Knights of Labor—then a secret society. Chalked signs on the sidewalks notified them of its meetings. Two of her sisters were dressmakers. Because of these family responsibilities my mother did not marry until she was thirty years old—an "old maid" in those days.

My mother was always interested in public affairs. She early became an advocate of equal rights for women. She heard many lecturers in Concord—Susan B. Anthony, Frances Willard, Frederick Douglass, Dr. Mary Walker, a pioneer medical woman, and Charles Stuart Parnell, the great Irish orator. She shocked her in-laws and neighbors by having women doctors in the nineties, when her four children were born. This was a radical step some sixty-four years ago, not long after Dr. Elizabeth Blackwell had opened up the practice of medicine to women. I was named after our doctor in Concord—Dr. Elizabeth Kent. I remember her when she vaccinated me to go to kindergarten—a handsome woman dressed in a tailored suit, the first I had seen. In Manchester, Mama also had a "foreign doctor"—an elderly French-Canadian woman who drove up in her own horse-drawn "buggy."

My mother admired women of intelligence who did "worthwhile things" in the world. She rebelled against the endless monotony of women's household tasks and remained at work in the tailoring establishment after her marriage as long as she could get caretakers for her children. This too was unusual in the nineties. She was an excellent cook, she liked to bake pies, make preserves, raise plants, but she hated what she called drudgery—washing, ironing, cleaning, dishwashing. She was happiest when she was sewing. She made over her green silk wedding dress into dresses for us to go to school. During her lifetime she made dresses for her three daughters. In 1913 a Paterson newspaper accused me of wearing an expensive imported linen dress to a strikers' meeting. Mama had made it for me at a cost of $3.00. The last beautiful dress she made for me was in 1937 when I spoke at my first Communist meeting at Madison Square Garden. It was of black velvet and she sewed it all by hand because at her advanced age of seventy-seven she could not run the machine.

Mama was no model housekeeper. But she was interesting and different and we loved her dearly. She read widely—newspapers, magazines and books. After we came to New York City in 1900, she went to night school to improve her penmanship and spelling and to hear lectures on Shakespeare. All during our childhood she read aloud to us—from Irish history, poetry, fairy stories. I recall one of her favorite books was on Greek mythology, *Gods and Heroes*. She had a large set of paper-covered volumes called "Classics and the Beautiful." We have a precious collection of books which were always *"Mama's Books."* They include a five-volume set of Irish literature, volumes of Burns, Moore, Byron, Whittier, Sheridan, Swift, Mrs. Browning, Mrs. Hemans, Meredith, Longfellow, Synge, Yeats, Lady Gregory, Stephens and Shaw.

When she was nearly eighty, she read from William Z. Foster:

"My father, James Foster, was born in County Carlow, Ireland, of peasant stock. He was a Fenian and an ardent fighter for Irish independence." She commented aloud to us: "My great grandfather, John Gurley, also came from County Carlow; so did George Bernard Shaw's grandfather, James Gurley. They were brothers. Shaw's mother's name was Elizabeth Gurley. The Larkins also came from there!" She went on reading, leaving us quite overwhelmed with this information. Finally I said: "Mama, why didn't you tell us this before?" She calmly replied: "The occasion never arose."

WE FINALLY ARRIVED IN New York City at the turn of the century—in 1900. My mother was tired of moving around and decided here we would stay. Our school terms had been interrupted and what little furniture we possessed was being smashed up in moving around. We came to Aunt Mary, a widow and a tailoress, who lived with her five children in the South Bronx. Soon they found a flat for us nearby. It was on the inside facing an airshaft, gaslit, with cold water. The only heat was the kitchen stove. We three older children cried, we refused to unpack our toys, and were as heart-sick for the green hills of New England as any lonely immigrants for their pleasant native lands. We missed the fields, the flowers, the cows, and beautiful Greylock Mountain we had seen from our window. We hated the big crowded dirty city, where now our playgrounds were empty lots with neither grass nor trees. The flats where we lived, at 833 East 133rd Street, are still in use, for "welfare families," I understand, although for a while they were condemned and boarded up.

We were horrified, too, at the conditions we had never met in our travels elsewhere—the prevalence of pests in the old slum houses—mice, rats, cockroaches and bedbugs. My poor mother carried on a desperate struggle to rid us of these parasites. And then something horrible happened to us in school—pediculosis is the scientific term—"lousy" the children called it. One child can infect a whole classroom, as every teacher knows. Yet often you will hear a smug prosperous person say: "Well, at least the poor can keep clean." I remember my friend, Rose Pastor Stokes, answering a woman who said this: "Did your mother ever look at a nickel in her hand and decide between a loaf of bread and a cake of soap? Well, mine did!" To be clean requires soap, hot water, changes of underwear, stockings and handkerchiefs, enough sheets and pillow cases and heat in the bathroom. We had none of these in periods of stark poverty. Mama washed our underwear clothes at night to be ready for the next morning.

On cold winter days we'd huddle in the kitchen and shut off the rest of the house. We would do our lessons by a kerosene lamp, when the gas was shut off for non-payment. We'd undress in the kitchen, scurry to the cold bedrooms, all the children sleeping in one bed, where we put our coats over us to keep us warm. We might as well have lived on an isolated farm in the Dakotas for all the good the benefits of the great city did us then. Bill collectors harassed my gentle mother—the landlord, the gas man, the milk man, the grocer. Once she bought us an encyclopedia, on the installment plan. But she couldn't keep up the payments and our hearts were broken when we lost the beautiful books we treasured so highly.

Our front windows of this long tunnel-like apartment faced the smoky roundhouse of the New York, New Haven and Hartford

Railroad. The great engines would chug in day and night and blow off steam there. Many railroad workers lived in the area. In particularly bad times they would throw off chunks of coal and then look the other way when local children came to pick up coal around the roundhouse. There were many accidents to railroad workers. Widows lived around us who had lost their husbands on that dangerous road, and their children starved while the road fought sometimes for years against paying damages.

There were many small factories, veritable sweatshops in the neighborhood, where children went to work as early as the law allowed and even younger. They made paper boxes, pencils, shirts, handkerchiefs (at three dollars a week and bring your own thread). There were larger factories employing adult labor—piano and refrigerator factories, a drug plant, and others. Mothers worked too and many children were left alone. Sometimes babies fell out of windows; one boy was killed when a huge sewer pipe rolled over him; a widow's only son fell from a swaying pole in a backyard, where he was putting up a clothes line and was killed. Children lost legs on the railroad and under trucks on the streets. The wife of the corner saloon-keeper made huge kettles of soup for free lunch and sent bowls of it around to the poorest families. People helped each other as best they could. Truly, as some philosopher said, "Poverty is like a strange and terrible country. Only those who have been there can really speak of it with knowledge."

An unforgettable tragedy of our childhood was the burning of the excursion boat, the *General Slocum*, in 1904. It had left the Lower East Side loaded with women and children on a Sunday school picnic of the Lutheran Church. When it reached Hellgate, a pot of fat upset and the kitchen took fire. The captain tried to reach a dock at 138th Street. By then the boat was an inferno. A thousand people died as a result of burns or drowning. The local undertakers' establishments were full of bodies. The Alexander Avenue Police Station was a temporary morgue, where grief-stricken fathers and husbands rushed up from the East Side to claim their dead. It was heartrending to all of us in the neighborhood, like a disaster in a mining town. Investigation showed that the boat was an old firetrap, with inadequate fire-fighting equipment and life-preservers. The captain, who did his best, was sent to prison, which cleared the company of responsibility for negligence. It was considered one of the worst marine disasters up to that time. The lives of working-class mothers and children were sacrificed to greed and corruption.

Life in the South Bronx

Childhood casts a glow around some events, even in poverty. It was a great day when we moved one block, from 133rd Street to 511 East 134th Street, on the corner of Brook Avenue. We lived there for twenty-seven years and a whole book could be written around "511," our lives there and our famous visitors. It was a sunny corner flat facing south, but gaslit and without hot water for many years. We never had steam heat, though electricity was finally installed. In the last few years, at our own expense, we put a small fireplace in the parlor, which helped to heat the house. We also installed a porcelain tub. As the old tin tub was being carried out, our very nearsighted landlord stood on the stairway. Thinking it was a coffin he stood respectfully bareheaded as it passed.

Our long residence was a record, in a neighborhood where for years families got one month's rent free, paid a few months, stayed on a few more until they were dispossessed, and then moved on, to repeat the same procedure elsewhere. When we moved in, there were red carpets on the floor and shiny brass door knobs and mail boxes. But it became more and more dilapidated with the passing years and each new, indifferent landlord.

Our windows looked out over the Harlem River and Manhattan's skyline. We saw the Hellgate Bridge in construction. We liked the friendly noises of the railroad—the whistles at night, the red glow of the engines, the late night milk-trains rumbling in, and sometimes the circus cars from Bridgeport. One night in the midst of a political argument a crony of Pop's looked out the window and said: "My God, Flynn, is that an elephant?" Pop replied: "It must be the beer!" But it really *was* an elephant, out for a stroll from a circus car. We loved to see the fire engines clatter down the hill from Brown Place, the horses' hoofs striking sparks from the cobblestones. Once there was a terrible fire opposite our house, on Brook Avenue. Three tenement houses were burned out late at night, in zero weather. Over twenty families rushed out in their night clothes, to escape the flames. They lost everything—their poor furniture and meager clothes. Everyone around opened up their stores and houses, took the victims in, fed and clothed them. They made wash-boilers of coffee and piles of sandwiches for the firemen, who were there all night. Hoses froze and had to be thawed out. One pretty girl on our block met a handsome fireman that night as she gave him coffee, and they were married later—a romantic finale to that memorable fire in a working-class district.

In New England we had bought wood by the cord and coal by

the ton. But here, in the South Bronx, we bought coal in bushel bags and wood in little bundles, which were three for five cents at first. This was sold by "Joe," the only Italian in the neighborhood. In the summertime he sold ice, and wine all year round, if he trusted you. There was only one Jewish family for many years, that of Mr. Isaacs, who kept a pool room. My mother insisted we treat him courteously, though others did not. She approved of his place, which she said he ran like a social hall for the boys and the neighborhood, and it kept them out of trouble. She was firm in teaching us respect for other people's nationality, language and religion. Most of our neighbors were German and Irish. The Germans owned the stores. The saloons were owned by the Irish. Italian women, with colored handkerchiefs over their heads, shawls over their shoulders, and great circular earrings, would come up from Harlem to the open fields in the Bronx to pick dandelion greens, which they carried back in great bundles on their heads. In the evenings, Italian laborers would walk back over the bridge, on the way home from work. The children threw stones at them and shouted "Dago." As little children, in Manchester, New Hampshire, and Adams, Massachusetts, we had lived near Polish and French Canadians, who were called "Polacks" and "Canucks." My mother would tolerate none of this and would say firmly, "How would you like to be called *Micks*?"—as the Irish were for so many years.

In the early days of our life in the South Bronx, at the turn of the century, there were no amusements for children, or for adults, either. There were no movies—the nickelodeon started later—no radios, no television, not even the old-fashioned phonograph, which also came later, and by now is a museum piece. Reading was our sole indoor pastime, especially in the long winter nights. We walked over the Willis Avenue Bridge to the East 125th Street library for books. We read everything we could understand, and some we did not, including all the traditional books of childhood of the day—Louisa Alcott, *Alice in Wonderland, Robinson Crusoe* and Fenimore Cooper, Walter Scott, Mark Twain, George Eliot, and the New England poets. My mother was a kind but reserved woman. She did not allow us to go into other people's houses; she frowned on over-familiarity and gossip. But she was a good neighbor in time of need. She helped the sick, advised on domestic problems, and when she baked pies and cakes she shared them with the neighborhood children. It was a calamity to the area when she moved away to Brooklyn in the late twenties. My father ran for N.Y. State Assembly in 1918, on the Socialist ticket. He got over 6,000 votes and ran ahead of the Republican. But lots of people said: "Too bad it wasn't Mrs. Flynn that was running. She'd easily get elected! Everybody knows her!"

Doris Kearns Goodwin

WHEN I PICTURE my mother, Helen, she is sitting in her favorite cushioned chair and she is reading. She was slim and tall, several inches taller than my father. Her hair, primly curled with the soft waves of a permanent, was brown touched with gray. She never wore shorts or even slacks. In the grip of the worst heat waves, she wore a girdle, a full slip, and a cotton or linen dress with a bib apron perpetually fixed to her shoulders. Such modesty was the norm in our neighborhood. Indeed, when one of the mothers took to sitting on her front lawn in a halter top and shorts, her behavior startled the block.

My mother had a long face, conspicuously marked by the deep creases and the furrowed brow of a woman twice her age. When she was in her thirties, she was told by her doctor that she had the arteries of a seventy-year-old. Shortly after I was born, she had undergone a hysterectomy after being diagnosed with cancer.

Though it turned out that she did not have cancer, the removal of her ovaries and her uterus had precipitated a surgical menopause, which, in those days before hormone replacement, rapidly escalated the aging process. In addition, the rheumatic fever she had suffered as a child had left her heart permanently scarred.

When I was two, she began having angina attacks six to eight times a year, episodes characterized by severe pain on her left side and a temporary loss of consciousness. All we could do, the doctors told us, was break smelling salts under her nose to restore consciousness and leave her on the floor until the pain subsided, which sometimes took several hours. I can still remember the chill I felt from a place so deep within me that my entire body started to tremble when I first saw her stretched out on the floor, a pillow under her head, a blanket over her body. My father assured me that everything would be all right, and said I could sit beside her for a little while and hold her hand. After these "spells," as we euphemistically called them, she would quickly resume her household routine, allowing us to imagine that all was well again.

In our family album there was a photo of my mother in her early twenties, sitting in a chair in her parents' home, her long legs thrown casually over the arm of the chair, her lips parted in the beginning of a smile. Twenty years after that photo was taken, there was in her halting gait and nervous expression scarcely a trace of her former vitality and charm. I used to stare at that picture and try to imagine the high-spirited person she was before I was born, wishing that I could transport myself back in time to meet the young Helen Miller.

Every night, I would fall asleep with the prayer that while I slept the lines on my mother's face would vanish, the leg that now dragged behind her would strengthen, her skin would lose its pallor. During my waking hours, when seated alone, I would daydream, allowing my imagination to reshape those realities I did not wish to accept. In my fantasy, my mother would appear as the young woman in the photo, wearing a summer dress with a ribbon in her hair. She was no longer short of breath, she could run and skip and dance. All my neighbors were crowded together on our lawn to watch my mother jump rope. My friend Eileen Rust and I each held one handle of the striped rope while my mother counted aloud the number of times she could jump without stopping. She jumped and jumped until she reached one hundred, two hundred, and then five hundred, and still she kept going. The strength had returned to her arms and her legs, her cheeks were red. The sun was shining and the wind was blowing, and I was so happy I could hardly breathe.

It was, however, through the older, frailer Helen, not the young woman of my wishful imaginings, that I came to worship the world of books. Whereas my father's interest in reading was confined mainly to newspapers and magazines, my mother read books in every spare moment: books in the middle of the night, when she had trouble breathing; books in the morning, after she cleared the breakfast table; books in the early afternoon, when she finished the housework, shopping, and ironing; books in the late afternoon after preparations for dinner were completed; and, again, books in the evenings.

The corner drugstore had a lending library where current bestsellers could be rented for several cents a day. And in the center of our town stood the cramped public library she adored, an old brick building built before the town had a high school or a bank.

With linoleum tiles on the floors, a massive receiving desk, ladders reaching the top shelves, and books spilling out from every corner, our library held a collection begun more than a decade before the village itself was incorporated in 1893. The books my mother read and reread—*Jane Eyre*, *Wuthering Heights*, *Anna Karenina*, *Tales of the South Pacific*, *David Copperfield*—provided a broader, more adventurous world, an escape from the confines of her chronic illness. Her interior life was enriched even as her physical life contracted. If she couldn't change the reality of her situation, she could change her perception of it; she could enter into the lives of the characters in her books, sharing their journeys while she remained seated in her chair.

Every night, after I brushed my teeth and settled into bed, my mother came to read to me. I loved listening to her voice, so much softer and less piercing than mine. She read slowly and deliberately, lingering over the passages she liked, helping me to feel the rhythm of the language, the pleasure in well-chosen words. She modulated her voice to reflect the different characters and the pace of the narration. Rudyard Kipling was one of my favorite writers. I took to heart the motto of the ever-curious mongoose family in "Rikki-tikki-tavi"—"Run and Find Out." Everything was investigated firsthand; hearsay meant nothing. If there was an inkwell on the writer's desk, then Rikki-tikki's whiskers would be stained with the blackest India ink; if there was a rustle in the garden, Rikki-tikki's eyes would glow with anticipation.

From the *Just So Stories*, I learned how the camel got his hump, how the rhinoceros got his skin, and, best of all, how the elephant got his trunk. At the start of the story, the elephant had only a bulging nose, no bigger than a boot, incapable of picking up anything. Just as I identified with the intrepid mongoose, so I empathized with the elephant's child, full of a "satiable curiosity" which irritated everyone around him. He asked the ostrich why her tail feathers grew, and the ostrich spanked him. He asked the hippo why her eyes were red, and the hippo spanked him. He asked everyone what the crocodile ate for dinner and, finding no answer, ventured to the riverbank, where he ended up in the crocodile's mouth. His friend the snake hitched himself around the elephant's hind legs and told him to pull as hard as he could to save himself, and as the little elephant pulled, his nose began to stretch and kept on stretching. By the time the crocodile finally let go, the elephant had a full-grown trunk. Thus curiosity was abundantly rewarded.

The young Thomas Edison, like the elephant, the mongoose, and me, was relentlessly curious. I had come to know him through the Blue Biography series, which my mother read to me in its entirety. Written for children, this classic series focused on the childhoods of famous Americans, including Abraham Lincoln, Susan B. Anthony, Benjamin Franklin, George Washington, Betsy Ross. But Edison, so full of energy and elaborate plans, fascinated me the most. At one point, he decided to read all the books in the town library, one shelf at a time, something I could easily imagine wanting to do myself once I had learned to read. And he, too, was always questioning his parents and teachers. He wanted to know why he saw lightning before he heard thunder, why water couldn't run uphill, why some parts of the ice pond were lighter than others.

But I suppose my fascination with Edison was fueled by the knowledge that when my mother was sixteen she had worked as the private secretary to the president of the New York Edison Company. It was her first job after graduating from secretarial school. I pictured her walking swiftly through the streets of Manhattan in tailored clothes with high heels, to take her place behind a big desk in a tall building. In my imagination, she worked directly for Thomas Alva Edison himself, as his gal Friday. I envisioned her at Edison's side in his laboratory when he invented the phonograph and the electric light. She would try to set me straight on chronology, informing me that she hadn't even been born when these inventions were made, but I refused to let her corrections disrupt the dramatic narrative I was writing in my head. Every year, on the eleventh of February, Edison's birthday, I made up Alva buttons for the family. I cut out circles of poster board and pasted a picture of Edison on the front with the name "Alva" in big red letters along the top. The name "Alva" intrigued me, and I liked the thought that my mother knew him so well she would call him by that exotic name.

The only joy that surpassed listening to a book read aloud was listening to real stories of my mother's youth. "Tell me a story," I would beg, "a story about you when you were my age." She told me stories about her father, who was a ferryboat captain operating between Weehawken and Hoboken; stories about her mother, whose parents had emigrated from England, and her uncle Willy, also a ferryboat captain, who had fought in the Great War and traveled halfway around the world. There must have been some money on my maternal grandmother's side. My mother always referred to the house she grew up in as "the Mansion," and she talked about an uncle who was a successful artist, who did all the frescoes for the famous Hippodrome theater on 43rd Street in New York City.

She told me about her twin brothers, who died at the age of

two during a cholera epidemic that swept through New York in 1906, shortly before she was born. The two little boys were laid out on a cherrywood table in the parlor of her parents' home. Ever after, when I passed the elegant table, which now stood in the corner of our dining room, I pictured two round-faced cherubs waiting in heaven for the rest of their family to join them. Thus the table became, not a reminder of death, but a platform to paradise.

I pressed her to tell me every detail about her first meeting with my father. "The first time I saw your father, he was standing at the door to our house. He had come to pick up my brother, Frank, who was his best friend." I wanted to add to her story, to have her tell me that the moment she saw him she knew that this was the man with whom she wanted to spend the rest of her life. Unfortunately for the story I was spinning in my head, she was only fourteen when they first met. "But what about Dad? He was nineteen, right? Didn't he know the first time he saw you?" "Perhaps." She smiled. "But it was a few years before he stopped thinking of me as Frankie's kid sister and realized I was a young woman. We were friends first and only later fell in love. That's the best way, I think." I nodded agreement, though I could never completely give up the notion that romantic love struck like a bolt of lightning.

As we talked about the past, she seemed to forget her pains. Her eyes brightened, and when she smiled, the creases at her mouth turned upward, giving her face a look of relaxation and warmth it did not usually have. I came to believe that, if only I could keep her youthful memories alive, if I could get the happy thoughts of her girlhood to push the sadder thoughts of her womanhood away, I could prevent the aging process from prematurely moving forward. In my imagination, the brain was a finite space with room for only a certain number of thoughts, so it was critical to push the bad thoughts out to leave space for the good ones. And somehow, on the strength of the changed expression on my mother's face, I assumed there was a direct correlation between one's inner thoughts and one's outer well-being. It made me so happy to see contentment on her face that I reached out to stories of the time she was young and vital as if they were lifeboats that would carry my mother through the present into the future. Through her stories, I could imagine her young again, taking the stairs two at a time. Even now, when I interview people for my books, it sometimes seems I am sitting with my mother pleading, "Tell me a story."

As a child, I loved looking through my mother's photo albums. Through a series of faded pictures attached by sticky corners to the pages, I discovered Ephraim and Clara Miller, the maternal grandparents I had never known, and my uncle Frank, who had died a few years before I was born. My mother told me she had considered her mother her "best friend in the world." When she worked at Edison, they spent every Saturday together. They would go shopping, eat lunch, and go to the movies. After my parents married and moved to East 64th Street in Brooklyn, my mother's parents moved into a house on East 63rd Street. When my sister Charlotte was born, my grandmother virtually lived at our house, helping to care for the baby, cook the meals, and keep my mother company. I stared at the pictures of my grandparents, both heavy people with kindly smiles, and imagined what our life would be like if they were living next door. I had never met either one of them, for they had died, suddenly, within three weeks of each other, when they were in their early fifties. My grandfather died first, of a heart attack. Three weeks later, my grandmother went into postoperative shock after what should have been routine gall-bladder surgery. She died the following morning. My mother was only twenty-two at the time.

One day, while my mother and I were looking through the album, she was called to the phone. In her absence, I decided that the pictures needed a little brightening. Taking my crayons, I colored a photograph of my mother and grandmother taken when my mother was in her teens, my grandmother in her forties. Standing side by side, they squinted in the sun, arms resting comfortably on each other's shoulders. With my red crayon, I gave my grandmother rosy cheeks and big lips and then colored her hair yellow so it would match mine. When my mother came back and saw the picture, she was so angry she could hardly speak. "But she looked so pale," I tried to explain, having no idea what I had done to make my mother so upset.

FROM *Shadow Man*

MARY GORDON

MY MOTHER IS SPEAKING FROM THE DESERT

MY FATHER IS dead, but I do not live among the dead. It is among the living I must move, even when they are touched by him, or the idea of him. It is their words I must respond to and to them I must speak.

There is, for example, my mother. My father's wife.

When I speak about my father, people often ask me, "But where was your mother in all this?" I don't know what to say. She was there, of course. And yet she wasn't with us. I don't know where she was.

As I don't know where she is now. She seems to be speaking from the desert. Everything she says now is spoken from the desert, a desert she has in part created. But only in part. Mostly, I suppose, the desert was created because she is eighty-six, and something has hardened, or broken, or worn out. The part she made came about through a dark will and a sense of worthlessness. Believing she deserves nothing, she surrounds herself with empty air. The sun gleams in her eyes. Her eyes can sometimes seem colorless, as if they were ruined by looking at the sun. Sometimes she looks blind. Her eyes are very beautiful. The rest of her face is gaunt now, and so you must look at her eyes: you can't look at anything else.

When she hasn't combed her hair, when she has a lost tooth she won't have attended to, when she won't cut or file her nails or change her clothes, she is distressing to look at. She used to be a very buoyant person, fleshy, with a wonderful skin that always made you think of the inner flesh of fruit: an apple or a peach. When she wore sleeveless dresses in summer, the cool thick muscles of her upper arms made you want to rest your hot cheek against them. The freshness and crispness of those dresses was a miracle. Their colors were the colors of nature: sea-green, sky-blue. It was as if she were wearing the elements themselves—the limitless sky, the refreshing sea—instead of a dress made of material whose shade was only a reminder of sea or sky.

In winter she wore hats with feathers, and tailored suits made of men's fabric, with shoulder pads and serious straight skirts. She "went to business." She was a legal secretary. She worked for one lawyer from 1937 to 1970, when he died; then she became his partner's secretary. She was proud of her business clothes, different from the clothes of mothers who had nothing at stake in what they wore; they could slop around the house wearing anything, and what would it matter? In her handbag she carried a gold compact and lipsticks that smelled like nothing else except themselves but that

I knew would taste delicious if only I could taste them. I wanted to taste everything: her skin, warmed or cooled by a light dusting of freckles, her light dresses, her lipstick, her perfume.

This was the body that my father knew and loved and took in marriage. This was the body upon which he engendered me.

But underneath this freshness, this crispness, this robust, delightful not only health but healthfulness, there must always have been a secret devotion to rot. Perhaps it had to do with the polio that struck her at the age of three. Buried beneath her grief and shame about her body, and beneath the stoicism that conceals her grief and shame, like a softening tuber underneath a field.

Now the healthfulness is gone; she has burrowed down to a deeper place, a darker place, perhaps one she feels to be more truthful. Or perhaps, thought of another way, it is a place she goes to in the desert. The place of carrion. She lies down beside it, she makes her home in it: there she is at peace.

Would my father lie down beside her? And where would there be a place for me?

She has lost her memory. As I am obsessively involved with bringing back my father from the past, she is letting the past slip from her hand, a fish into dark water. She is letting it drop through a scrim of tissue paper into the night air. She is allowing it to disappear in snow.

She is in a nursing home now. If I come upon her now when she isn't expecting me, I find her sitting with her head buried in her hands. There is no need for her to do anything now but adopt this formal posture of grief. Yet I don't think she wants to die. She will not, I believe, die soon. She has, I have been told by many doctors, the heart and blood pressure of a teenager.

If I were an allegorist, if I decided to do something in the manner of Giotto, embodying the virtues in a human figure, I would paint my mother in her wheelchair, her head in her hands, wearing her magenta sweater (the only one she wears, although there are a dozen in her cupboard). I would call it "The Death of Hope."

She hopes for nothing, and because I believe that nothing can be done for her, because I have given her up, I hope for nothing on her behalf. Now everything in her life points out the futility of hope. But if I had wanted to paint Hope, the embodied virtue, I would have painted my young mother in her sea-green or sky-blue dress, her lovely arms, her white skin, and her strong and useful, perhaps rather dangerous, teeth. Because hope can be dangerous, in that it leads to the death of hope. But it does not lead in a straight path to death. There is the animal, with the animal's hope. This is not human, it is not our own. It is something, but it is not ours.

THERE IS A LINK between hope and memory. Remembering nothing, one cannot hope for anything. And so time means nothing. It is a useless element. Living in time without memory or hope: a fish in air. A bird in water. Some unfortunate creature doomed to the wrong medium. Yet not, alas, to death.

I don't know what my mother does all day. She eats her meals. She sleeps.

I know that she prays. But I don't know what she's doing when she prays. What is she saying? Where is she? Is she in a blank silence, the presence of God, where there is nothing without meaning and she knows she is where she has always belonged, perhaps where she has always been? Is she silent, or is she saying words to God? Her own words or the formal words of prayer? Or is she having simple conversations, too banal to repeat, yet placing her exactly at the true, safe center of the universe? She says she prays for me. She says she prays for me and my family all the time. I believe her. But I don't know what she is thinking of us when she prays. Or even who she is thinking of, since she sometimes forgets that she has grandchildren.

I think she must be happy, praying. Or at least not suffering, in a place beyond memory. She is in a place that was the center of her marriage. What brought my parents together was their understanding that the Catholic Faith was the most important thing in their lives. Because they both believed this, and I don't, they can go somewhere that I can't follow. I'm excluded once again, as I was when they closed the bedroom door.

When my mother prays, she's once again what she often was: outstanding. I believe she sees the face of God. But who can see the face of God and live? Who can see the face of God and remember it? Perhaps that's the point. Perhaps it's the point most especially for my mother, for the way she must live now. The ways she has no choice but to live. Praying, she comes alive. Free of her body. Beautiful again: a spirit. Joyous. Not weighed down. Not even tragic. Partaking of greatness. Great. With God, outside time, so that memory is irrelevant, the anguish of its loss erased.

* * *

BUT WHEN SHE'S FINISHED praying, her loss of memory becomes an anguish once again. I take her to a doctor at Mount Sinai to see if there's anything she can do that might reclaim her memory, return her zest for life. The doctor asks her questions.

She answers with words from the desert. "I don't have my memory anymore. I don't think about things. They were all sad."

The doctor, who is beautiful and lively and wonderfully intelligent, says gently, "What about the happy things. Do you think about your husband? You had happy times with him."

She says she doesn't remember him. But she does remember her mother. She remembers being a daughter, but not a wife.

If she doesn't remember my father as a husband, then another part of him is lost. The history of him as a husband. The history of them as a couple.

They were introduced by a priest, and then they courted, in some way I don't understand, for several years. When she was thirty-nine and he fifty-three, they became engaged. People who knew them said they were almost embarrassingly amorous, for middle-aged lovers. They necked on the subways for everyone to see. Occasionally, they would kiss in front of me, full on the mouth, like people in the movies. I would pretend to think it was all right, but I would have to force myself not to pry them apart, not to stand between them, not to stop them. Which I'm sure I could have, if I'd only tried. But I knew it was important that they seemed to be kissing like people in the movies, because most of the time they didn't seem happy with each other. Most of the time, they fought. They fought about money.

When I heard them starting to fight, I would run upstairs to the attic. Upstairs, away from them, I felt free—what had money to do with me or I with money? I stood beneath the bare beams, in the emptiness, watching the gold light strike the bare wood floor in straight vertical shafts. I would sing loudly so I couldn't hear what they were saying. "I won't give you one red cent for carfare." "You should get your head examined." I twirled around and around, pretending my skirts were long and billowing. I thought the dust motes traveling down the shafts of light were a blessed substance, like manna. I was privileged to be in proximity to it, but I would never dream of following the light upwards to its source.

The attic was meant to be our storage place, but we had nothing to store. My mother had taken nothing from her mother's house and my father had lived nowhere: in spare rooms of other people's houses, in hotels. The people who had owned the house before our landlords were named Chamberlain. "English," my father said. Meaning: "Protestant: nothing to do with us." I associated those bare beams, that clear light, and all that space with Protestants. Chamberlain. The clear sound, the clipped off consonants, the relaxed polysyllable. No need to rush or argue for the Chamberlains. They'd left behind a beer stein on one of the attic windowsills, a black background, green figures in salmon-colored pantaloons and black tri-cornered hats. I never touched it. I believed that if I touched it, the Chamberlains would never come back. I longed for them to come back and give me retroactive permission to inhabit their attic. Perhaps they would move in there with me: I could imagine the sun striking their blond hair. Sometimes, I'd look out the window and imagine I could see them walking up the street. I'd never met them, but I knew I'd recognize them the first moment they appeared.

From the attic, I could hear my father and the radio. WQXR:

The Radio Station of *The New York Times*. I'd sneak up on him and tease him for conducting a phantom orchestra. He'd told me that music was very important, not just the songs my mother and I sang. My mother and I loved singing songs from musicals, and songs from the twenties. Cheerful songs, always with upbeat, bouncy rhythms, "When the Red, Red Robin Comes Bob, Bob, Bobbin' Along" and "Tiptoe Through the Tulips." My father couldn't sing. He said that one day I would play the piano, like his mother. He ripped a picture of Beethoven out of the encyclopedia and hung it near my toy box at a level where I could see that imposing head when I was trying to play my games. The only other picture in the house was his print of Holbein's *Thomas More*. No landscapes, no still lifes, no pretty children in ornate hats. There were photographs of ourselves, as if we were movie stars that we admired.

I think that our idea of ourselves was taken from the movies. Certainly, my mother must have got the idea for her marriage from the movies, or at least the courage to defy her parents and move away from home at the age of thirty-nine with a strange, unsuitable man. And we behaved more like people in the movies than like the people we knew. My mother and I sang; my father and I danced to the radio. We all did imitations and told jokes. We made fun of stuck-up people. We went out to eat.

Our familial ideal was from a particular kind of movie. It never included midwestern families around the dinner table; our treasured models were connected not to small towns or farmlands but to show business or crime. Our particular favorites were childless couples who lived in penthouses; food prepared and consumed inside the house was of no importance in our lives, as it wasn't for them. My parents took pride in this. "Why do you have concern for what you put in your mouth?" Jesus had said, "It goes into the belly and ends up in the drain." My parents thought they were living by these words of Jesus, but it wasn't eating that displeased them—it was cooking, and setting and clearing the table, that they didn't like. We were happy going out to eat, then going to the movies. But when we came home from the movies, my parents would begin to fight again.

No one remembers any of this now. If I ask my mother anything about my father, or our life together, she just looks confused. Not only is my father dead to her, the memory is dead. I am the only heir to a still-living memory.

THE DOCTOR WHOM I take her to see about her problems with her memory asks her questions on what is a standard diagnostic test for depression. But we run out of time and the doctor suggests that perhaps I could ask her the questions and simply circle the answers on the form. These are the questions:

Are you basically satisfied with your life?
Have you dropped many of your activities and interests?
Do you feel that your life is empty?
Do you often get bored?
Are you hopeful about the future?
Are you bothered by thoughts you can't get out of your head?
Are you in good spirits most of the time?
Are you afraid something bad is going to happen to you?
Do you feel happy most of the time?

Do you often feel helpless?

Do you often get restless and fidgety?

Do you prefer to stay at home rather than going out and doing new things?

Do you frequently worry about the future?

Do you feel you have more problems with memory than most?

Do you think it's wonderful to be alive now?

Do you often feel downhearted and blue?

Do you feel pretty worthless the way you are now?

Do you worry a lot about the past?

Do you find life very exciting?

When I first ask her the questions she answers everything positively. She is satisfied with her life, she isn't bored, she's hopeful, she's in good spirits, she doesn't worry. I think I understand something. I ask her if she thinks that saying there's anything wrong with her life means that she's complaining, that she's ungrateful for what she has, that she's a weakling, a cry baby. Of course that's what I think, she says, looking at me from the desert. I tell her that's not the way it is; they need to know how she really feels for their work. It's their business to get an accurate picture, I tell her. "You have to do it for them." I never tell her who "them" is and she never asks. "Okay, if it's their business," she says.

She answers the questions slowly. She isn't satisfied with her life, she isn't happy, she often feels helpless, she often feels downhearted and blue, she feels her situation is hopeless. She frequently feels like crying. On the other hand, she doesn't feel that her life is empty, she is hopeful about the future, she is not afraid that something bad is going to happen, she thinks it is wonderful to be alive. Her most heartfelt response is to the question "Do you feel pretty worthless the way you are now?" "Oh, yes," she says, "completely worthless." She is speaking from the desert. She is looking at me with those eyes burned by the sun. There is no softening landscape. No hidden refreshing spring. The dry land. The harsh rock. The sky, unmediated. When I start to cry she says, "What are you crying about? How else would I be?" And I tell her all the wonderful things she's done, how much she's been treasured and loved. "That was then," she says. "I thought you were talking about now."

WHEN I CALL THE doctor and read her the results of the test, she says my mother is on the border between dysphoric and depressed. She thinks my mother might be helped with antidepressants, but the chances are slim. She'd like to have an M.R.I. done on my mother, because some of the neurological signs were a bit confusing.

I don't tell my mother that we're going for a test that is frightening, claustrophobia-inducing. I don't tell her till a day before that she's going to have a test at all. I try to describe the procedure to her. They put you into a kind of tube. You're a bit shut in, but if you relax it's quite bearable. I tell her I had one myself, and that I fell asleep during it, which was true. I decide to take her on the city bus, which provides access for people in wheelchairs, because the first time we went to the doctor, we waited an hour and a half for the ambulance going, two hours coming back. "They've got you over a barrel, and they know it and they don't care," the woman at the nursing home tells me. I think how pleased I would be to firebomb the ambulance headquarters; the relief of seeing the place and the people go up in flames.

On the bus, I understand that not having a memory makes my mother ashamed. The shame of the bankrupt. She pretends she remembers things. "Oh, yes, I remember these people. I've seen them before. Their faces are familiar." On Madison Avenue in the Eighties, where she has never been in my lifetime, she says, "I remember this was where we used to get off." I can't imagine she was ever on a Madison Avenue bus. When she was young, she came to the city to go to the theater, or the rodeo at Madison Square Garden. She loved the rodeo; when it was in town she went to it every night. She had some dates with rodeo cowboys, whose names remained dear to her. Turk Greeneau and Cecil Henley. Turk married Sally Rand, the fan dancer, who was famous for causing a stir at the 1933 Chicago World's Fair. My mother always said, with real indignation at the loss to the rodeo world, "She broke his stride for good." If I laughed when she said that, she'd get angry. I wonder if my father knew about the rodeo cowboys, and was jealous. I remember that he ripped up a copy of *Photoplay* that my mother had bought for the picture of Gary Cooper.

She also regularly went to a retreat house on Twenty-ninth Street where she'd met my father. Or to Saint Patrick's Cathedral. Everything I know of her history makes me sure that she was never on the Upper East Side. And I know she's never seen her fellow passengers. I have to fight my desire to tell her, "You're wrong, you've never been here before." I wonder if she thinks she's been on these streets and seen these people before because all people and places are the same to her. Memory enables a sense of difference. The present is different from the past. The remembered event is different from the current experience, the difference is recognizable, and therefore the events can be differentiated.

Is everything for my mother in the present? Does she live like God?

Does she live like my father?

The loss of memory brings some mercy. By the time we get to the hospital for the M.R.I. my mother's forgotten it. So she's experienced no anticipatory dread.

The technician tells her to lie completely still, or the pictures will be useless. After a few minutes, I see her beginning to thrash. Through a microphone the technician tells her in an accusing voice that she is ruining everything. Instantly, I know what to do. I jump up, run over to the hole her legs are sticking out of, and thrust my head in. "We're going to say the Rosary," I tell her. And into the hole I shout, "The five sorrowful mysteries, the first mystery, the Agony in the Garden." Our Fathers. Hail Marys. The second mystery. The third. She settles down and lies quietly. The test is done. I realize that for me, who claims to live by words, there are no words that could automatically take away my terror. No poetry, no passages from great novels, could be shouted at me and cause me to lie still. She is, in this way, more fortunate than I.

When we get to the doctor's office, on the other side of the Medical Center, the doctor asks my mother if the test was difficult. What test, she asks. The doctor describes the M.R.I. I don't remember anything like that, she says.

Another piece of good fortune; without memory there is no reliving of terror. The past no longer haunts. It is finished, and for good.

* * *

BUT IF A LOSS of memory spares pain, it also vexes questions of pleasure. How is pleasure judged if it cannot be relived, recalled? It seems, from a capitalist stance, a bad investment. What yields pleasure yields it at some cost. Time, effort, money. Particularly in her case, since she is immobile, she must be brought to things or things must be brought to her. If she is brought to something, the effort is enormous. When I think of doing things that might please her, I often find myself asking, "Is it worth it?" Worth what? The effort. Also, the resentment the effort entails. The capitalist's resentment for a bad investment.

What is something worth if it doesn't lodge in memory? Take, for instance, my son's Christmas play. I'd had a meeting with the social worker, the nurse, the doctor, who are in charge of my mother. We all agreed that she'd been less responsive than formerly. We agreed, as a team, to be more hopeful, more inventive, more persevering in suggesting things that might bring her "out of herself." None of us asked where she might be when she was in herself. As I left the meeting, I was inspired to ask my mother if she'd like to see her grandson as the star of the Christmas play. Usually, she says no to everything; she hasn't been out of the nursing home in three years. But for some reason, she said yes.

I move with extreme efficiency. No ambulette is available. An ambulette makes it possible to wheel her into a van; she doesn't have to get out of her wheelchair. But we're not lucky; all that's left is a regular ambulance, which, I find, requires that she be lifted off her wheelchair onto a stretcher. The two attendants, both very young, one a slight Hispanic with an even slighter mustache, the other a chunky, opulently permed Italian, are both charming, help-ful, and kind. My mother likes them; she flirts with the young man; she tells the young woman she's half Italian. We go up Broadway, sirens flashing. We arrive at the school and she's wheeled in on a stretcher. The sea of parents parts for us. The attendants switch her from the stretcher to a wheelchair. David, my son, introduces her to his teachers, the head of the middle school, and all his friends. When the play begins, the drama teacher says that David has asked that the play be dedicated to his grandmother. She loves everything: the Christmas carols, seeing her grandson in a major role (as Chico Marx), the dedication, all the attention. She glows with happiness as she is transferred from the wheelchair to the stretcher. We sing Christmas carols in the ambulance on the way home. I leave her at her room; she says she'll certainly sleep well tonight.

I am in love with her, with myself, with everyone involved in the evening. I tell myself that I have to do more things like this, all it takes is imagination and hopefulness and a little thought. What a difference can be made by things like this, I say, as I fall blissfully to sleep.

In the morning, I call her. I say, "Did you wake up thinking about last night?"

"What happened last night?" she asks.

"The play," I prompt her. "David's Christmas play."

"I don't remember. I don't remember anything," she says.

My first thought is that she's done this to make a fool of me. No, to make a fool of hopefulness. Then I think that it was such a wonderful experience for her, and she knew how rare it would be, so she had to forget it so as not to long for more things like it. Then I think that it doesn't matter, the experience is lost, it is worse than if it never happened. All the effort, all that expense. I vow I won't tell my son. I hope he doesn't bring it up if he sees her, or that she'll have the sense to fake it. With all my will I remind myself that she was happy at the time, that that's what matters, that it's not important that she doesn't remember it. For the moment, it was of great value; I tell myself we live for moments only. But I don't believe it for a second.

I think about this when it comes time for the spring Shakespeare play. David is playing Falstaff. I tell her I'll come and get her on the bus; the bus trip to Mount Sinai was easy enough, and it's the difference between a fare of five dollars and an ambulance fee of two hundred dollars. But when the morning comes, I am reluctant to do it. I think of what a good friend has told me, that since things mean so little to her, I shouldn't make extraordinary efforts for her. I should do what is easy for me, and pleasant for both of us. I shouldn't do anything that taxes me, anything that I'll later resent and be angry with her about. He says I have to realize the truth about the way she is: that nothing I do matters anymore.

Most of the time I don't realize it. But the day of the play is overcast and humid. I focus on how rude the bus driver was to us on the way home from Mount Sinai, how I had to fight with him to pull the bus near enough to the curb, how I lost my temper, screamed at him, filled out a complaint. Bus drivers don't like stopping for wheelchairs; they don't like getting out of their seats, moving the necessary bench, opening the lift mechanism with the special key. They don't like locking the wheel of the chair into its special clamp. This makes me hate them.

On the morning of David's play, I wake at five-thirty to write about my father. It doesn't go well. All morning I am terribly fatigued. I begin writing and reading well only at noon. I am reading Beckett's *The Unnameable*. If I take my mother to the play, I have to stop writing and reading at one-thirty. If I don't, I can work until three.

I very much want to read and write. I keep remembering the episode of the Christmas play, the episode of the M.R.I. I think how hot it is, how difficult it will be to push the wheelchair up the hill on Eighty-sixth Street, between West End Avenue and Broadway. I think of the bus driver's inevitable distaste. I read a sentence of Beckett's: "Close to me it is grey, dimly transparent, and beyond that charmed circle deepens and spreads its impenetrable veils." I remember that four days ago my mother said, when the doctor asked her, that she had no grandchildren.

I decide not to take her. I decide that what it will take out of me is greater, much greater, than what it will give her. I'm just too tired to.

I call and say I have a bad back, which I do, and that I'm afraid pushing the wheelchair up the hill might hurt my back. Which it might. It also might not. I've decided the chance isn't worth it. Which means I'm giving up on her again. Giving her up. Allowing her to fall through the sheet of tissue paper into darkness. Since it seems to be what she wants. Since I no longer have the faith to go after her. Since I would rather write about her than push her up the hill. Since I need to save my strength to find my father, who is waiting somewhere, somewhere I do not know. I know exactly where she is. I always have. There is no need to look for her. I must force myself to look at her. Force myself to resist the impulse, as strong as any in my life, to turn my face when I see her face.

FROM *The Autobiography of Mother Jones*

MARY HARRIS "MOTHER" JONES

I WAS BORN IN the city of Cork, Ireland, in 1830. My people were poor. For generations they had fought for Ireland's freedom. Many of my folks have died in that struggle. My father, Richard Harris, came to America in 1835, and as soon as he had become an American citizen he sent for his family. His work as a laborer with railway construction crews took him to Toronto, Canada. Here I was brought up but always as the child of an American citizen. Of that citizenship I have ever been proud.

After finishing the common schools, I attended the Normal school with the intention of becoming a teacher. Dressmaking too, I learned proficiently. My first position was teaching in a convent in Monroe, Michigan. Later, I came to Chicago and opened a dressmaking establishment. I preferred sewing to bossing little children.

However, I went back to teaching again, this time in Memphis,

Tennessee. Here I was married in 1861. My husband was an iron molder and a staunch member of the Iron Molders' Union.

In 1867, a yellow fever epidemic swept Memphis. Its victims were mainly among the poor and the workers. The rich and the well-to-do fled the city. Schools and churches were closed. People were not permitted to enter the house of a yellow fever victim without permits. The poor could not afford nurses. Across the street from me, ten persons lay dead from the plague. The dead surrounded us. They were buried at night quickly and without ceremony. All about my house I could hear weeping and the cries of delirium. One by one, my four little children sickened and died. I washed their little bodies and got them ready for burial. My husband caught the fever and died. I sat alone through nights of grief. No one came to me. No one could. Other homes were as stricken as was mine. All day long, all night long, I heard the grating of the wheels of the death cart.

After the union had buried my husband, I got a permit to nurse the sufferers. This I did until the plague was stamped out.

I returned to Chicago and went again into the dressmaking business with a partner. We were located on Washington Street near the lake. We worked for the aristocrats of Chicago, and I had ample opportunity to observe the luxury and extravagance of their lives. Often while sewing for the lords and barons who lived in magnificent houses on the Lake Shore Drive, I would look out of the plate glass windows and see the poor, shivering wretches, jobless and hungry, walking along the frozen lake front. The contrast of their condition with that of the tropical comfort of the people for whom I sewed was painful to me. My employers seemed neither to notice nor to care.

Summers, too, from the windows of the rich, I used to watch the mothers come from the west side slums, lugging babies and little children, hoping for a breath of cool, fresh air from the lake. At night, when the tenements were stifling hot, men, women and little children slept in the parks. But the rich, having donated to the charity ice fund, had, by the time it was hot in the city, gone to seaside and mountains.

In October, 1871, the great Chicago fire burned up our establishment and everything that we had. The fire made thousands homeless. We stayed all night and the next day without food on the lake front, often going into the lake to keep cool. Old St. Mary's church at Wabash Avenue and Peck Court was thrown open to the refugees and there I camped until I could find a place to go.

Near by in an old, tumbled down, fire scorched building the Knights of Labor held meetings. The Knights of Labor was the labor organization of those days. I used to spend my evenings at their meetings, listening to splendid speakers. Sundays we went out into the woods and held meetings.

Those were the days of sacrifice for the cause of labor. Those were the days when we had no halls, when there were no high salaried officers, no feasting with the enemies of labor. Those were the days of the martyrs and the saints.

I became acquainted with the labor movement. I learned that in 1865, after the close of the Civil War, a group of men met in Louisville, Kentucky. They came from the North and from the South; they were the "blues" and the "greys" who a year or two before had been fighting each other over the question of chattel slavery. They decided that the time had come to formulate a program to fight another brutal form of slavery—industrial slavery. Out of this decision had come the Knights of Labor.

From the time of the Chicago fire I became more and more engrossed in the labor struggle and I decided to take an active part in the efforts of the working people to better the conditions under which they worked and lived. I became a member of the Knights of Labor.

One of the first strikes that I remember occurred in the seventies. The Baltimore and Ohio Railroad employees went on strike and they sent for me to come help them. I went. The mayor of Pittsburgh swore in as deputy sheriffs a lawless, reckless bunch of fellows who had drifted into that city during the panic of 1873. They pillaged and burned and rioted and looted. Their acts were charged up to the striking workingmen. The governor sent the militia.

The railroads had succeeded in getting a law passed that in case of a strike, the train crew should bring in the locomotive to the roundhouse before striking. This law the strikers faithfully obeyed. Scores of locomotives were housed in Pittsburgh.

One night a riot occurred. Hundreds of box cars standing on the tracks were soaked with oil and set on fire and sent down the tracks to the roundhouse. The roundhouse caught fire. Over one hundred locomotives, belonging to the Pennsylvania Railroad Company, were destroyed. It was a wild night. The flames lighted the sky and turned to fiery flames the steel bayonettes of the soldiers.

The strikers were charged with the crimes of arson and rioting, although it was common knowledge that it was not they who instigated the fire; that it was started by hoodlums backed by the business men of Pittsburgh who for a long time had felt that the Railroad Company discriminated against their city in the matter of rates.

I knew the strikers personally. I knew that it was they who had tried to enforce orderly law. I knew they disciplined their members when they did violence. I knew, as everybody knew, who really perpetrated the crime of burning the railroad's property. Then and there I learned in the early part of my career that labor must bear the cross for others' sins, must be the vicarious sufferer for the wrongs that others do.

These early years saw the beginning of America's industrial life. Hand and hand with the growth of factories and the expansion of railroads, with the accumulation of capital and the rise of banks, came anti-labor legislation. Came strikes. Came violence. Came the belief in the hearts and minds of the workers that legislatures but carry out the will of the industrialists.

IT WAS ABOUT 1891 when I was down in Virginia. There was a strike in the Dietz mines and the boys had sent for me. When I got off the train at Norton a fellow walked up to me and asked me if I were Mother Jones.

"Yes, I am Mother Jones."

He looked terribly frightened. "The superintendent told me that if you came down here he would blow out your brains. He said he didn't want to see you round these parts."

"You tell the superintendent that I am not coming to see him anyway. I am coming to see the miners."

As we stood talking a poor fellow, all skin and bones, joined us.

"Do you see those cars over there, Mother, on the siding?" He pointed to cars filled with coal.

"Well, we made a contract with the coal company to fill those cars for so much, and after we had made the contract, they put lower bottoms in the cars, so that they would hold another ton or so. I have worked for this company all my life and all I have now is this old worn-out frame."

We couldn't get a hall to hold a meeting. Every one was afraid to rent to us. Finally the colored people consented to give us their church for our meeting. Just as we were about to start the colored chairman came to me and said: "Mother, the coal company gave us this ground that the church is on. They have sent word that they will take it from us if we let you speak here."

I would not let those poor souls lose their ground so I adjourned the meeting to the four corners of the public roads. When the meeting was over and the people had dispersed, I asked my co-worker, Dud Hado, a fellow from Iowa, if he would go with me up to the post office. He was a kindly soul but easily frightened.

As we were going along the road, I said, "Have you got a pistol on you?"

"Yes," said he, "I'm not going to let any one blow your brains out."

"My boy," said I, "it is against the law in this county to carry concealed weapons. I want you to take that pistol out and expose a couple of inches of it."

As he did so about eight or ten gunmen jumped out from behind an old barn beside the road, jumped on him and said, "Now we've got you, you dirty organizer." They bullied us along the road to the town and we were taken to an office where they had a notary public and we were tried. All those blood-thirsty murderers were there and the general manager came in.

"Mother Jones, I am astonished," said he.

"What is your astonishment about?" said I.

"That you should go into the house of God with anyone who carries a gun."

"Oh that wasn't God's house," said I. "That is the coal company's house. Don't you know that God Almighty never comes around to a place like this!"

He laughed and of course, the dogs laughed, for he was the general manager.

They dismissed any charges against me and they fined poor Dud twenty-five dollars and costs. They seemed surprised when I said I would pay it. I had the money in my petticoat.

I went over to a miner's shack and asked his wife for a cup of tea. Often in these company-owned towns the inn-keepers were afraid to let me have food. The poor soul was so happy to have me there that she excused herself to "dress for company." She came out of the bedroom with a white apron on over her cheap cotton wrapper.

One of the men who was present at Dud's trial followed me up to the miner's house. At first the miner's wife would not admit him but he said he wanted to speak privately to Mother Jones. So she let him in.

"Mother," he said, "I am glad you paid that bill so quickly. They thought you'd appeal the case. Then they were going to lock you both up and burn you in the coke ovens at night and then say that you had both been turned loose in the morning and they didn't know where you had gone."

Whether they really would have carried out their plans I do not know. But I do know that there are no limits to which powers of privilege will not go to keep the workers in slavery.

Trinity

KERRY HERLIHY

HERE ARE THE things everyone wants to know:

1. I have always known I was adopted.
2. I have wonderful loving parents.
3. I searched for ten years and found my birthmother, Mary.
4. I look like her.
5. She has six kids who don't know I exist.

I'm on a big plane, bigger than I've been on since I was about nine years old. The difference between then and now is I am alone. My mother is not with me to show me where we are flying over or to wake me up to get my breakfast. I have that panic that bubbles below words and ration. It is the same thing I felt when I had to share a locker with someone I didn't know at the YMCA on Saturday mornings. I would cry and attempt throwing up to get peaceful again. When my mother would try to rescue me from my tears, I would just wish she would know and make it go away. I still wish for that magic, but no one appears.

I decide I must find a friend before I get to St. Louis, but it doesn't work out. No one sits next to me, and the man two seats over falls asleep within forty-five seconds of sitting down. I actually think of waking him up because these are extenuating circumstances, but then I look at him, lose my nerve, and decide maybe I should pray even though I haven't prayed since the last time I flew.

Now, as always when I get on planes, I forget my qualms with the Catholic Church. Instead, I focus on the saint I like. The Virgin. I talk to her when I interpret turbulence as an engine failure, and am convinced that my salvation is close at hand. Hail Mary becomes my mantra. This morning, I keep repeating Hail Marys as best I can remember. It calms me and focuses my mind and heart.

The captain interrupts me. "We are now beginning our initial descent into St. Louis . . ."

An invisible fist punches a hole in my stomach. I want to throw up. I go back to praying: "Holy Mary, Mother of God. Pray for us sinners, now and at the hour of our death. Amen."

I realize I left a part out about the fruit of thy womb. I forgive myself for that under the circumstances. Thinking about the fruit of any womb right now is a bit much. The plane heads down, and the hole in my stomach becomes a cavern. I think about starting another Hail Mary but really focusing on getting the words right. However, the countdown has begun: fifteen minutes to birthmother. Ten years of searching. A lifetime of keeping two beginnings and two identities separate. My mother's voice is clear in my head, "I am glad that you have organ donors now." I try to remember Mary's voice, but she fades in and out like a low, deep frequency—a formless buzzing that hits my bones. I feel sick again.

I say my name to myself. Kerry Anne. I like that name. My mother likes that name. She came up with it in a pinch when my father was set on naming me Eunice. Thank God she understood the legacy of a name. If my father had had the final say, I don't want to even imagine where I would be. Mary says she likes Kerry Anne. She says it suits me. She wrote that to me several weeks ago. I am happy she mentioned my name but wonder what it means when she doesn't even know who I am yet.

I say my other name. My name at birth. The name Mary gave to me before she gave me up. Patricia Margaret. I form the letters and try to make it exotic and new. The problem is I have two cousins and one aunt named Patricia and God only knows how many Margarets lurking in my family tree. Each time I try to make that name me, all I see is the annual Fourth of July family party with all my relatives sitting around eating potato salad and green Jell-O mold. I love Irish names, but I just wish there were a few more to go around. At best, Patricia Margaret feels like an imaginary friend I outgrew but still talk about. Usually she slips away from my attempts to get her closer to Kerry Anne.

I have three photos of Mary. One of her by herself, blowing out a cake that reads, "Happy Birthday Mom"; one of her and her husband, Pete; and one of her with Pete and their six kids. I spread them out and wonder how I fit in. On the other hand, I wonder how those photos fit into the hundreds, maybe thousands of family shots that tell the story of who I am. I place the picture of Mary next to one of my mom and wonder if, under different circumstances, they would be friends.

I give up on Hail Marys at this point, because I realize my brain cannot separate the Virgin Mary from Mary who I am about to meet at the gate. Instead, I think of my six orange toenails that I painted perfectly last night at 2:00 A.M. when I insisted to myself that I was absolutely fine. They are symbols of serenity as these crossroads loom closer.

At toe number six, I decided I needed to start packing. I kept remembering my mother, giving me advice on what I could and could not wear. No green boots. No baggy pants. Wear a belt. Lipstick to give your face some color. My mother who feels her mothering is represented in this outfit. She has called me several times this week but didn't want to talk about Mary. In fact, she often refers to her as "that woman" or just plain "her." I wonder what my mother is feeling as she is trying to support me and also wonder how the story, our story, my story, ended up taking me on a plane away from her to St. Louis twenty-seven years after it began.

The plane drops and my stomach goes with it and I wonder if this is like having a baby. Probably not, but it's traumatic nonetheless. I hear the wheels pop out, and now I really wish I was with my mom in the ocean by our house in Maine and this could be just another story I tell about myself that didn't end with this descending plane and this moment that I can't put away behind the laughter or words. I wish I'd listened to my grandmother more and could say the 23rd Psalm, which she said was what you should rely on in dire circumstances. I resolve to buy a Bible the minute I get back to New York so I won't be stuck in a jam like this again. I put ten Chiclets in my mouth as the wheels touch down in St. Louis.

I realize this is the moment of intersections. These are my last moments of controlling this story. Whatever happens from this point on must be shared.

The FASTEN SEAT BELT sign goes off, and I exhale loudly. I want the man next to me who has just woken up to ask me something. It really doesn't matter what, because as long as I am prompted, however vaguely, I'll spill the beans. I was so protective of this meeting. No cameras. No tape recorders. No friends. No family. Just me. Now, I would give anything to have someone I love holding my hand and telling me to spit out the Chiclets. I cough loudly, thinking if the man next to me thinks I am choking he surely will say something. He is preoccupied and ignores my dramatics. He gets up and moves to the aisle. Holy Mother of God. I have to get up now. I am here now. I am a corridor away from meeting my birthmother. I practice my smile in the plane window, trying to see my reflection.

After letting about four aisles behind me get off, I gather my things and walk. I feel suspended. I walk like I am a normal person until I get to the middle of the corridor and freeze. Where are my glasses? What if I miss Mary because I can't see her? I fumble frantically and drop my book and Walkman. My glasses are missing. I convince myself that I have left them on the plane or back in New York and wonder how bad it would be not to get off the plane. I wonder if birthmothers have abandonment issues too or if it is something different altogether. My hand hits the metal frames, and I know it is now, not next week, not next month. Now. I don't feel ready, but that doesn't seem to move me any farther away from my story. And so I go.

I see her immediately and start to cry. I know that it is predictable that I am crying, but it also bewilders me. In my adoption search, there has always been a distance between the story I tell and my connectedness to it. Even at this moment, I can't go to those deep places without shooting back to the surface. I hug Mary and look around to see if any sensitive person has picked up on the significance of this hug. No one is paying any attention. I realize we are both shaking.

She has this vaguely familiar face that I think I should know. As we walk to sit down, we keep sneaking looks at each other, like lovers, tentative, curious, and hopeful.

You look like me, I say.

The gene pool is pretty strong.

We sit and stare at each other, and then Mary asks me about my mother.

What does your mother think about all this?

I think for a moment and decide not to tell her that my mother forbade me to bring any baby pictures although she couldn't say why. "I just don't want her to have them," she stated.

It is hard, I say simply, and hope she will understand.

Mary nods her head. We talk about the strangeness of what my mother is being asked to do. Somehow we both feel comfortable here. I can feel my mother's sadness in my bones even though she is 1,000 miles away. If I were home, she would call me in about thirty seconds because she can just tell when I carry her with me. I wonder if Mary has that same connection with her daughter.

What do you want to know? she asks.

All the questions that have waited, bursting for all these years, dissolve. I realize that part of this story is still, like my panic, below language and questions. I figure I have to muster something, so I ask what I have heard many people ask me: Any health issues?

She shakes her head and says no, except that her father was an alcoholic.

Before I can stop and because it makes some kind of sense, I say that my grandfather was an alcoholic too. I immediately regret it because I know my mother would kill me. I have known Mary for less than five minutes, and I am already talking about my alcoholic grandfather. Somehow, I think she might understand. When I think of my grandfather, I smell red raspberries behind his house, where I learned how to pick fruit without crushing the perfect center. This somehow lives in harmony with the drinking my mother tried to hide from me. I think because Mary is Irish, she will know this without my having to explain it all.

We talk for another hour over lunch outside the airport. She tells me her son and his wife live here. Since only her husband knows about me, I wonder if she is scared about bumping into anyone she knows. I get a thrill out of being a real live secret. It gives me an edge knowing that I embody someone's sordid past. Until this moment, I never thought the word *illegitimate* applied to me. Adopted or illegitimate, I didn't think it was possible to be both.

Mary drops me back at the airport. She asks me if I feel better, and I say yes. I am happy to be heading for home. Before I get back on the plane, I call my mother and tell her how it went. She is happy I am not hysterically crying or overly enthusiastic about Mary. I tell her I still love her best.

MY MOTHER IS VISITING me in New York for my birthday. It is technically the weekend after my birthday, but I decided to take a whole week to celebrate my twenty-eighth year. My friend Helen told me twenty-eight is when the planets are in the same alignment as when you were born, and it is a significant passage.

My mother and I are on the subway to Brooklyn when she asks, "Did you hear from Mary?"

I want to tell her I've been pissed off for two weeks because I have heard nothing since we met, and I was the one who sent *her* a very nice card. My friends keep taking her side, saying she is probably overwhelmed. When I am not in yoga class actively trying to be a better person, I want to tell her, Get over it. I am a pretty good catch. She should be singing hallelujahs and sending me care packages on a weekly basis. What Mary doesn't seem to understand is, she is getting in the way of my happy ending. It is all very logical:

Long, arduous search with appropriate number of dead ends, local Midwest historians, hysterical frenzies, identity crises, and moments of drama. Check.

Tentative letter to birthmother and first return phone call. Check.

Exchange of photos and letters as prelude to meeting. Check.

Tearful and heartfelt reunion. Check.

Frequent but not overbearing use of greeting cards, notes, and phone calls to develop a close and satisfying relationship that in no way replaces the wonderful mother I already have.

Still waiting on that one, thanks to Mary.

I don't tell my mom any of this. I just say, "I haven't heard from her since we met."

"Good," she says.

I look at her, and she knows I know there is a lot underneath that one word.

After a minute, she adds, "I wonder about her every year on your birthday. I wonder what she thinks and how hard it must be for her."

I feel guilty because she makes me realize I have never, not even once, thought about Mary on my birthday. Though it makes me feel selfish, I am happy my mother and Mary shared something without me. I wonder if Mary and my mom will ever meet. Another thing to put on the checklist. Way down.

We get home, and I check my mailbox as we go inside. As I open the box, I can see a card with Mary's return address on it. Luck of the Irish. The one day my mother is with me to check mail is the exact day Mary's card arrives. I shove it between the junk mail and act like everything is normal. I know I can't read it in front of her, but I have to see what is inside that card. Fortunately, I am not a well-prepared host and there's nothing to eat in the house. After I put my mom's things in my room, I tell her I'm going to run out and get some snacks. I slip the card slyly in my coat pocket and get out the door unnoticed. I feel like I am having an affair. I rip open the card. It is a birthday card. I open it and read Mary's note.

Dear Kerry,

Although you haven't heard from me, you've been in my thoughts since we met. I guess I am still overwhelmed. It was such a joy and blessing to see the woman you've become—confident, self-assured, mature enough in the love of your parents to take the risk to find and contact me—more than I could have ever wanted for you—my thoughts and feelings are still a bit jumbled but time will sort things out—

Know that you are in my prayers as you always have been, but especially on your birthday—M.

I reread the card, and my diatribe wilts in its wrath. It's funny she finds me confident and self-assured when all the doubtful demons swirl furiously within me. I like her adjectives though. Not quite a Hallelujah Chorus, but I'll take it. I wonder how much time we will need to make this real.

I want to run back and let my mother be the first person I tell about Mary's card. But I don't. There is loyalty, guilt, and the fiercely guarded love I have for her. I am *her* daughter. I slip the card back into my pocket and head for home.

Charting Life with a Daughter

MAUREEN HOWARD

WHEN I WAS growing up, one of the sights in town was a mother-daughter team in matching outfits, both their heads clipped in girlish bobs. They walked miles each day through the department stores and busiest streets on an endless shopping trip, totally absorbed in each other—talking, talking, talking down the years.

The mother's face was not a touch more wizened than her daughter's in the end: a mirror image, the daughter aged to her mother's gray. They had successfully closed out the world yet they felt the need to parade their sad attachment. The memory of those two crones haunts me as my daughter pushes toward sixteen and we look at the goods at Bloomingdale's and jabber on about espadrilles.

We get on pretty well. The arguments about pierced ears and mascara, even the wrangling about French homework, seem to be behind us. I don't envy her youth or her particular talents; I know she doesn't find me a hopeless case. We size each other up constantly—the same round Irish faces—and I'm convinced that with our uncanny similarities we have consciously entered into a stage that will go on forever, of defining ourselves apart. Neither one of us will pack a suitcase and run off, but for all our camaraderie a kind of rebellion is implied for both of us.

On my part I resent all the middle-class niceties that she insists on—good note paper, the table correctly set for company. She has put a great effort into teaching me how to fold napkins into perfect little dunce caps but I refuse to learn. My daughter cannot possibly realize the years it has taken me not to care about matched towels or a neat refrigerator.

Then again, I'm intolerant. I can't believe that she can gobble Vonnegut and Joyce with equal appetite: What a terrible moral flaw—a thinness of spirit that may be corrected with time. I'm appalled that she can simultaneously have a crush on Sylvester Stallone and Peter Martins, an indiscriminate attraction to pectoral muscles for heaven's sake, while I've always leaned in the direction of the grand Fabian lady Beatrice Webb's proposition (equally faulty) that a woman should love the ablest men in her life. So we draw off into our separate corners.

COLETTE, WHO WROTE WITH such emotional accuracy about her mother, did not do well by the daughter whom she loved. It's one of the few times she fails. The stories of Bel-Gazou are tinged with a sweet, but false, attitude toward the girl's state of innocence. The child never grows up. By way of instruction I prefer Jane

Austen's adolescent heroines. Perhaps because she did not have a daughter, she saw the problems of growing up with clarity and wit. She has an affection but no excess of love for her clever girls. They are so ignorant and self-assured as they start on their journeys to moral awareness. The mothers or guardians in her novels, wise or foolish, are played off against the young women, but Austen is their real mother—scolding them, laughing at their folly, soothing their battered hearts until they are ready for adult lives. But literary models don't help me with my own child. The stories of Elizabeth Bennet or Emma Woodhouse flatten the reality of the two of us, face to face. Our physical presence is sometimes too much for us to tolerate in the same room.

I have noticed, during the past few years, that all my friends with teenage daughters go through a check list. Does yours have the record, the Earth shoes, the messy room? My best friend in England wrote to me last week—we have daughters the same age: After a quick run-through of news, her book about to come out, their plumbing reimagined, et cetera, there is an exultant bit about her girl. At last this beautiful, bright child, top of her form at St. Paul's, has a blow dryer and the new Kiss album. I'm guilty of playing this game all the time, and I think for women who openly care about their daughters, who have said all that we feel now about careers, about the value they must set on themselves—it's a way of still keeping them little girls. We chart their sexual and cultural development as we once compared their doll houses, relief maps of Egypt, stringbean plants growing on the windowsill. It is a relief to be amused by their adolescence. It scales them down, just as they can cut us down to size—our dowdy shoes, boring friends, martinis. Patronizing, yet sympathetic, we pursue what is "normal" in each other. It takes the edge off passion. And it faces away from particular failures we see in each other all too clearly.

It was not an easier day when there were rules of conduct and decorum for a mother to insist upon: Do not wear white gloves before Memorial Day. Still, in the midst of a demanding conversation with my daughter I'd often like to retreat to such absurdities: it is unladylike to cross your legs, or, the most foolish dictum that I've run across, in an etiquette book, circa 1870: "No young lady will be guilty of sucking the head of her parasol in the street." It would be a lot more fun to deliver that line than to continue, both of us somewhat embarrassed, about pot, liquor, or contraception, but we are stuck with being frank, aware.

WE SOUND ALIKE ON the phone. Neither one of us can spell. With a mutual telepathy, we steer away from the crazy lady on the bus. We even honor each other's secrets. I am sure my daughter knows exactly where I stash away my good blouses that I don't want her to wear to school. I discover the empty cigarette packs in her jeans. This was the child who, in first grade, pricked pinholes in my cigarettes and hid them in the freezer so I would give up smoking and I obeyed. It is ritualistic now when we get into battle. I think diamond earrings are vulgar on a kid. She will go to some vaguely chaperoned party that lasts through the night. We are still adversaries.

Time: 7:30 on a weekday morning. The hall of the apartment is littered with clothes. My daughter, Loretta, stands on the coffee table to get the full-length view of herself in the mirror over the couch. She has discarded five costumes. Biology class will be mostly over by the time she arrives at school. She is now wearing a flowered sundress, a canvas schoolbag and a large straw hat with velvet streamers meant for a garden party. I am obliged to tell her—the naysayer, killer of all fantasy and fun—with a sharp edge in my voice that the hat will not do for the subway ride to Brooklyn. She discards the hat, walks to the door and explains to me very nicely: "I understand that I will not always be this way." Nor will I.

Motherlove

CALEDONIA KEARNS

THE FIRST YEAR my parents were separated was the only year my father gave my mother regular child support. She saved it up and took us to Ireland. I was three, and one of my first memories is riding a gray horse in rocky Donegal. The trip is significant in my memory as it marked, in some symbolic way, the beginning of our life alone, without my father. My mother never remarried, and I remained her emotional center, her only child. If I were to take another name it would be Persephone—a daughter so beloved her mother's grief over her absence stopped the world. My engagement ring is a garnet for a reason. Like Persephone, I ate the pomegranate seed because I needed to get to a place my mother couldn't find me.

I grew up with a ghost. My mother and I lived alone together in five apartments, and I was sure my grandmother's spirit moved with us, taking up residence within our walls—she was our silent witness. It was not the breakup of her marriage to my father but her mother's death from breast cancer that haunted my mother. I knew her loss as it lived around me and within her. I don't remember a minute of my childhood when I wasn't aware that at any moment I could lose my mother. That her mother could come back to claim her and I would be alone.

The April of my twenty-fifth year, I found a lump in my breast during a routine physical. It was hard and round, a solid mass that moved from side to side like a nickel between my middle and index fingers. Actually, the doctor found it. She felt it and said, "Oh. What's this? I'm sure it's nothing." But I knew it wasn't nothing. I thought that was it. This time my mother was doomed to lose me too, to her mother's darkness. I feared her mother had come to take me, but as the anesthesia began to take hold I prayed and my grandmother came to take me under though this time she let me go. The lump was benign.

I have always known her. Worn my mother's sorrow as if it were my own. I will be married in my grandmother's wedding dress—the dress she borrowed from her sister during World War II to marry my grandfather because he was on leave. It is a forties dress with a ten-foot train. It makes me think of my grandmother in a knee-length skirt with heavy red lipstick being steered away by her sisters from the news flash in Times Square that the Japanese had bombed Pearl Harbor, where my grandfather was stationed. The dress is thick ivory satin and is the only thing besides my mother that has touched us both.

At this point, my fiancé and I have been together longer than my parents were. They were married in Greenwich Village, and my mother wore a crimson velvet bridesmaid's dress with her grandmother's lace veil falling like a mantilla over her head.

I hated that dress. It was red for one thing and did not fulfill my dreams of ivory. To me it represented my mother's rejection of femininity. I took ballet classes. She grew her armpit and leg hair. Her footwear, though it was to become a national trend, was humiliating to me. She has worn sandals of ugly brown suede for over twenty years. "You're so feminine," she would say, amazed at our difference when the contrast between me, blond and small boned, and her, full figured with dark hair, struck her.

Before she died, my grandmother said to my mother that if my mother would lose weight maybe there would be a miracle and my grandmother would be saved. As though her daughter's sacrifice could drive the cancer from her body. She made it clear that it was her daughter who could save her. I remember my mother's story of her junior year at college, the year her mother died, of driving to the store alone to buy pumpkin pies and pudding, of feeding herself excessively while her mother wasted away in an oxygen tent two hours away.

I think Persephone ate those seeds because she could not tell Demeter, her mother, that life with her was too much. She could not say out loud that her mother's love was like perpetual summer, all heat and blossoms with no periods of cool darkness. She couldn't stand only being her mother's daughter. She wanted to be somebody to someone else—anything—a lover or a wife? But Demeter got her back—mothers always do.

I always knew I was my mother's life. She still wishes she had had more children. So do I. Intense love can leave you gasping for air, wanting to dig yourself out of someone else to find *you*. I have wanted not to matter so much. Everything I have known is that I was wanted. There is no way out, and I am blessed. Blessed by a love so strong I have wanted to push it away.

She was hurt I decided to get married in Brooklyn—away from the life we made together in Boston, the place that was ours alone. But I wanted to go back to the place we moved from together on my fourth birthday. I wanted to claim it for my own. Related to her, but set apart. I couldn't have her alone walk me down the aisle. I am not leaving her for my husband. I won't be passed from one to another. "God bless the child who's got her own." I did and I mothered my mother and fought for my own life. And this is what she gave me. A sense that my life was my own to muddle through. I found love because my mother loved me so much that I could not accept less from another.

In "My Mother's Mother" by Edna O'Brien, a young girl says, "I thought how much I needed to be without her so that I could think of her, dwell on her, and fashion her into the perfect person that she clearly was not. I resolved that for certain I would grow up and one day go away. It was a sweet thought and it was packed with punishment." I did not leave to punish her yet, becoming a woman separate from her is one of the most painful things I have done. It required a certain heartlessness on my part, but that is one of the advantages of being the child—you are expected to put yourself first.

The summer after I graduated from college and was living at home was the summer of my mother's twenty-fifth college reunion; her mother had graduated from the same school twenty-two years earlier. She told me that sitting in the chapel at the reunion she felt her mother's presence for the first time since she died and it shook her. I could hear it in her voice and how vulnerable she was when she hugged me. I was surprised—my grandmother had been with us for years, and I could not understand how my mother had never felt her before. I imagined her so strongly I felt she lived through me, that my mother was given a daughter to replace the mother she lost. And I did her work. My grandmother was gone; I had to pick up where she left off.

I woke up in the middle of the night last year wondering what happened to the dress my grandmother was married in. The satin dress with the long train in the picture of my grandparents and their parents taken in 1943. It was stuffed in a plastic bag in the attic of one of my mother's cousins, and my mother and I drove out to Long Island to look at it—wrinkled but in good condition. We went to the town my mother grew up in, where her cousin still lives and her mother is buried. When the dress was pulled over my head, it fit like it was made for me.

On the way home, we stopped at my grandmother's grave. The flowers I planted last spring, my thanks for her answering my prayers the April of the lump in my breast, were coming up, pushing through cold ground.

What my mother says about her mother's death is that some days it feels like nothing and on others, more than thirty years after the fact, the grief rushes over her like it happened yesterday. I'm lucky I did not lose my mother, and together we survived my childhood. I count each passing year as grace. She is alive so I can push her away.

The Child as Houseguest

JEAN KERR

Now that I'm all grown up, I'll tell you what I want to be. A mother-in-law. For those interested in somber statistics, I will confess that I have been a *mother* for thirty years, a circumstance—I assure myself—that is hard to believe. We will dismiss as irrelevant the way I look in the early morning since I never appear *anywhere* in the early morning except, most occasionally, in the operating room of a hospital. (Of course, there they come and get you and sedate you and put you on a cart and wheel you down, which, we are agreed, makes it a lot easier.) But never mind my appearance. There are eight of us in this family and I'm the only one, so far, who's managed to get married—except, of course, for my husband.

It may be thought that my desire to be a mother-in-law has, perhaps, something to do with my wish to dandle a grandchild on my knee before I am too arthritic even to dandle. Not so, or, at least, not really. I don't think I'm a sentimental person. Certainly the salesperson in The Crystal Collage Gift Shop doesn't think so. I was hunting for my BankAmericard last week and she noticed the picture of a charming little boy in my wallet. "Which of your boys is that?" she wanted to know. And she seemed genuinely bewildered when I explained that the picture just happened to be the one that was in the wallet when I bought it.

However, I do admit that I find nothing in this world more joyous than the spectacle of an almost brand-new infant (five months is about perfect) who has just been bathed and sprinkled with Johnson's baby powder and snapped into a clean pink wrapper with his gauzy hair swooshed up into a little peak. No, I mean it. Nothing so lifts the heart—not getting good reviews on a play, not losing ten pounds, not even hearing the dentist say, "Well, we don't seem to have anything to do *here*."

But you can love something, yearn for it even, and realize it's no longer for you. Another example of the same thing would be Robert Redford.

By the time you're fifty—and why do I bring *you* into it, by the time *I'm* fifty—I'm not really looking to collect more children, however beguiling. I'm trying to unload. I don't mean get them out of the house. Except for one small girl, they *are* out of the house. Three of the boys are away at school (prep school, graduate school, medical school), and two are (oh, the wonder of it and I accept congratulations) actually employed and living in quarters of their own. But they don't belong to anybody else yet, they haven't been snatched, claimed, or taken over permanently by an alternate sponsor.

I don't know why young people don't seem to get married anymore. Unlike the Messrs. Gallup and Harris, I wouldn't recognize a trend if it sat down beside me. I do gather from the polls that theologians think it has something to do with the pill, while sociologists attribute it all to post-Watergate cynicism. Personally, I think the manufacturers of Brownie mixes have a lot to answer for. A boy hardly needs anybody else messing around in his kitchen these days.

Our friend Walter Slezak used to say, "Children eventually become letters and then the letters disappear," and I believed that. In fact, I got quite choked up about it. But I have learned that the facts are quite otherwise. In my experience, children *don't* disappear. They become houseguests. Lacking nests of their own, they turn up as often as meatloaf, arriving with the exuberant good cheer and frantic manner of tourists determined to see all of the Vatican Museum in twenty minutes. Certainly they don't want to be any trouble: "No, no, you sit down, Mom, I'll get my own sandwich." Presently a series of more or less connected observations can be heard from the deep recesses of the refrigerator. "I don't see anything besides this boiled ham. Are we out of mayonnaise? I'll tell you something, this lettuce has *had* it." Now this particular child lives in Philadelphia. What does he mean, are *we* out of mayonnaise?

It's not that I want to retire from parenthood like a bank teller gets to retire from bank telling. I don't want a gold watch or other retirement benefits. All I really and truly want to do is shut up. And don't tell me I *could* shut up; that's been explained to me. But if this is still their home, or at least where they store their old guitars, and I am still their mother, I am, much to my dismay, going to *sound* like a mother.

Recently one of my sons was being given the benefit of my expertise on nutrition ("Cold spaghetti for breakfast and chocolate-chip cookies for supper? That's crazy!"). Now he was perfectly polite (they're all polite) but he was staring heavenward with that tinge of melancholy and ennui that I myself assume whenever the announcer says "Stay tuned, we'll be back right after this message." Believing myself to be on the side of the angels and Julia Child (if that isn't redundant), I said to him, "If I don't tell you, who will?" His answer is worth repeating: "Hopefully, nobody." But how can I be silent? There is darkness to be lit, there are shoals to be avoided, and we no longer have Eric Severeid to lend a guiding hand.

No, other voices must be heard. But, you may ask, would an average, typical, pretty girl of twenty-three do better than I? She certainly would. How I shall rejoice some rainy night when I hear some other responsible person say to just one of my loved ones, "My God, you're not going out in *this* weather, in *that*!" or, to repeat another phrase rather abused around here, "Okay, you don't want to have it cut, but couldn't you *wash* it?"

Having said that children are like houseguests, let me count the ways in which houseguests differ from children:

1. Your authentic, invited houseguest does not call you collect at midnight and announce, "Hey, Andy and I will be there for dinner tomorrow night, right? . . . No, that was *Albie*, who had an identity crisis because his father was a psychiatrist. Andy is really a terrific guy, he just can't eat anything with egg in it. See ya!"

2. Your A-1 houseguest does not usually bring along his dirty laundry.

3. He seems to fit in better with the family. More than that, he writes such charming thank-you letters. Our friend Charles was here for five halcyon days not long ago. His conversation is bewitching, he wears his hair becomingly short, he is as tidy as a Trappist. When he returned home he wrote, "Darling Girl, nothing will ever be the same here at Wuthering Depths, but I have my Gallo port and my memories . . ." Of course, one doesn't look for this kind of felicity within the family. But wouldn't you think someone could scribble a couple of lines on a postcard: "Gee, it was great to see the whole gang again, and gosh, Mom, I've missed your hot biscuits." Now it should be clear to any rational person that my biscuits, which come frozen in a cardboard tube, are—and this is being as literal as you can be—nothing to write home about. But I am tired of being a rational person. I want to be showered with idiot compliments like those women in the TV commercials who, apparently, enthrall everyone in the immediate environment with their shrewd use of some new fabric softener.

Why can't those kids lie a little, now that they're adults?

FROM *A Likely Story: One Summer with Lillian Hellman*

ROSEMARY MAHONEY

A T THE POST OFFICE there was a letter for me from my mother, and when I saw her handwriting my heart was flooded with happiness and sorrow all at once. It was the most familiar handwriting in the world; each letter, the way my mother fashioned it, had a bigger meaning for me, as though the letters were scribbled somewhere within my head, on the underside of my skull. I saw the handwriting, and immediately, with no effort of recollection, I heard my mother's voice in my ear. I opened the letter, and a limp five-dollar bill fluttered out from within its pages. This was a habit my mother had got into while I was at school, a five or a ten once a week, and seeing the money now surprised me and made me sad. I could picture her sitting at her desk tucking the money into the letter and feeling good about doing it, even though it wasn't much money. It was less money, in fact, than she thought it was. The letter was written on the back side of my father's old stationery, embossed with his name and address: John P. Mahoney, M.D., 2100 Dorchester Avenue, Boston, Mass. 02124 Telephone CYpress 6-4000. There were boxes of this stationery stacked up in my mother's office. She couldn't see the point of throwing away good paper.

Dear Ra:

I've been thinking about you and your job. You're a wonderful girl, Ro, everyone can't be wrong. It's not easy to move forward, because risks are involved and it's always more comfortable to stay put. But I know you're ready to take on new challenges, and that's exactly how you grow. The rest of the times we're just on plateaus. You stretch yourself to go beyond your present tolerance, and growth can be endless. I don't think any of us is aware how far we can go. Learn everything you can there. Let Lillian play great lady; she doesn't have much time left to preserve that image. You can cater to her demands and at the same time preserve your integrity. Look on it as a great period for learning how to handle yourself and others. Never be afraid to speak if anything's bothering you, but do it calmly and straightforwardly.

. . . This is a good lesson in self-control for you. So often in life we are judged wrongly and there's nothing we can do about it, so you take deep breaths, realize you are right, and go on to the next thing. You would like everyone to know you are right because how we appear in the eyes of others does concern us somewhat, but basically it doesn't really matter if you know it. How to handle disappointments, how to deal with losing, are really excellent preparations for life . . . In a one-to-one situation, like yours with Lillian, no matter what the other person says you do or don't do doesn't make it true. Their say-so isn't half as important as what you know. You're good, Ra, so you'll do a good job.

You ought to relax and just be Rosemary. I certainly think you should
speak when it's appropriate. You don't have to be angry.

You'll never have such free time again to read, write letters, and
keep your journal. So do it. Be sure to read some every day. I'll try to
write often, just a few lines here and there.

Rose, I love you a lot.

Mom

Tears pushed up into my eyes, and I pressed them away with
the heel of my hand. I already knew my mother loved me. I knew
she loved me more, in fact, than she loved herself. She didn't have
to tell me. I already knew it, and I knew that what she said was
true. But it was easier to say than do. Just be you, she always said.
But what was that? On the back of the envelope I was about to
mail to my mother I scribbled: *Mom, today was my day off and I also*
got paid. I don't know what to do with the money. She said she made the
check out to cash for my sake, taxwise—or so she says. Is she lying? If I
cash it will she get the police on me and say I stole her money? Love, R.

I mailed the letter and wandered slowly down to the ferry dock
and stared at the boats in the harbor. The masts wagged softly,
and there were so many of them they were like a screen in the air
above the water. From where I stood I could see the roof of the
Mill House tower, its shingles so smooth they looked like thatch.
And I could see the stone jetty hooked around the harbor of sailboats like a protective arm. Gulls with bowling-pin bellies bobbed
and veered like tethered kites over the dock, their feet tucked back
and their yellow beaks slightly open and touched with a drop of
red at the tip, like blood. The big, black *Shenandoah* with its two
masts slanted slightly back looked unfazed by the wind. The black
woman who was usually sitting in the sand wasn't there. I missed

her; she was only one person, but whenever I saw her she seemed to fill up the beach. I stood there a long time, then headed back through the town in the direction of upper Main Street. I was sick of looking at trinkets in tourist shops, and I had nowhere else to go. I stopped at the library and looked at books and magazines for a while, then checked out *The Sun Also Rises* and reluctantly returned to the house. The footlights along the path to the front door were on, and in the wetness they threw off a wispy, drifting steam like glowing pots of incense. I hated the house from this side, it was plain and there was so little of it to look at—all you could really see was its flat top, like the roof of an old office building.

When I went down to the kitchen, Hellman was making her lunch and drinking a Bloody Mary. "Back already?" she said, glancing over her shoulder at me as I came into the kitchen.

I put my book on the table and held on to the bag with my blouse in it. My hands were wet and cold. "Yes."

She broke two eggs into a bowl. "Like some lunch?"

I stared at her back, surprised by the offer.

"I'm fixing some for myself," she said, turning her nose to look at me. "If you'd like to join me, you're welcome."

Was she inviting me to have lunch with her? Why was she doing that? It made me nervous. I didn't want to join her. I could say no, but what would I do then? Lie on my bed and stare at the ceiling while she sat out here by herself? That would look rude and a even little weird. I was trapped, like a cat clinging to a log floating down a river. "Okay," I said.

She broke two more eggs into the bowl and stirred. "We'll eat here."

There were ears of corn piled up on the counter, a basket of bread on the table, and beets from the garden boiling in a pot on the stove. She sipped occasionally from her glass as she made scrambled eggs. The walls of the glass were furred with soft clumps of red from the tomato juice. Hellman was at her nicest when she'd had a drink. Her face took on a melancholy softness and the slant of her eyes grew more acute and she moved even slower and was more predictable. Carrying a carton of eggs from the refrigerator, she moved with a blind, picking tactility, a crustacean's delicate clumsiness. Her thin neck was draped in soft, loose folds of flesh, like pale velvet, and, as always, the tops of her ears were hidden by her soft hair. Her naked earlobes were huge. I could see she was at ease; her voice had the absent, mumbling tone it sometimes achieved when she relaxed. I felt safer when she was a little drunk, and it wouldn't have mattered to me if Lillian Hellman drank an entire bottle of vodka. I took off my raincoat, threw it on my bed, went back into the kitchen, and offered to help her make the lunch. I didn't want to, but I knew it was polite to offer, especially when I would be eating it.

"Slice a few carrots, if you like," she said.

When I cut my thumb slicing the carrots she said, "All right?" and though the cut bled steadily and stung with a hard, blaring throb I said, "I'm fine."

"Not hurt?"

"No," I said, hiding the cut in a paper towel. "It doesn't hurt at all." I didn't want to tell her the truth. Now that I had my chance, I didn't want to tell Lillian Hellman anything. It was the only bit of control I had over her.

We sat at the table before our two plates and began to eat. "This is a fine, silly lunch," she said. She lifted an ear of corn to her mouth and raked the kernels off with her teeth. She chewed carefully, grinding the corn as if with a pestle. She raised her glass to her lips, slowly, carefully, as she always did, and I realized for the first time that she rarely wore earrings. Neither of us spoke for some time. Self-consciousness extracted all the flavor from my food, and lifting the forkfuls of beets to my mouth, chewing and swallowing, I was merely going through the motions. I was acting. But she seemed to enjoy every bit of what she ate, not looking up from her plate much, apparently not affected by my presence in any way, as though this was something we had been doing together every day for years. She chewed and swallowed with great concentration, her fork trembled in her hand as it levitated from plate to mouth, and when finally she spoke, her voice was wetly altered by some colorful scrap of corn or beet lodged in her throat.

"You're interested in France," she said, her hand rummaging in the bread basket like a crayfish picking over muddy rocks.

I looked up at her. What had made her say that?

Before I could respond, she pointed with her buttery knife to the library book on the edge of the table. "The books you're reading. They're about France."

The unexpectedness of this made me sit up straight in my chair. I stared at the book. "France?" I tried to think of the books she had seen me reading. *The American*, Colette's stories, and now this Hemingway book.

Hellman said, "Newman in Paris, Colette in the French countryside, Hemingway's France after the war."

I was startled. I hadn't noticed that connection at all. All I saw was that the books were about people and yet they were entirely different from each other; I didn't see them as connected. Which country the stories took place in didn't matter to me. This was a different way of looking at a novel, thinking it was about France. The whole thing had caught me off guard: she had noticed me. She saw what I read and knew that it was about France even before I did. Suddenly I felt stupid and nervous. I felt she was looking through my clothes, and I crossed my arms impulsively. Though I was not especially interested in France I said, "Oh, yes, I'm very interested in France."

"You've been there, yes?"

I hadn't been there, and I knew that if I said I had she would start asking me what I thought of it. "I've never actually been there," I said.

She looked at me and reached for the salt.

I had hardly been anywhere, and that seemed pathetic and un-sophisticated too. "But I've been . . . I went to Ireland. Once."

She lifted her tattered ear of corn to her mouth. "Pretty place," she said into the corn, munching and seeming unimpressed with Ireland.

I moved my fork from one side of my plate to the other. Ireland was better than nothing. "And I'm going again in the fall."

"Vacation?"

I told her I was going there to study. My school was letting me go for my senior year, paying for it with my scholarship money.

"Oh?" She nodded, registering some kind of understanding. "A whole year. I have an Irish friend. Annabel Davis-Goff. She's the wife of Mike Nichols. They'll be coming here. You'll meet her. She's Irish-English actually."

Irish-English. I was pretty sure that meant the woman wasn't really Irish, she was English and just happened to live in Ireland.

"What else do you like to read?"

"Flannery O'Connor," I said, blurting out the first name that entered my head.

"Hmph." She frowned and blinked for a minute. "You understand her?"

As soon as she said this I realized that if there was something you had to understand about Flannery O'Connor, then I definitely didn't understand her.

"I don't know," I said, trying to laugh it off.

"Very taken up with Christianity."

I didn't really notice the Christianity part, though I saw the preachers. It didn't matter to me if I didn't get it. I liked Flannery O'Connor. I liked the weird characters she described in her stories, the walleyed goons, the people with handicaps and infirmities saying mean and funny things. I got the jokes, the witty descriptions, the snappy ripostes. "I like Willa Cather," I said, "and John Steinbeck. And I like William Faulkner and Edith Wharton."

Hellman wiped her mouth with her napkin. "You like American writers," she said quickly.

Why didn't I notice these distinctions, these classifications? To me these writers were just people who told stories. It didn't occur to me that they were Americans. I felt like I had had a blindfold over my eyes, and suddenly I didn't want to talk about books anymore.

"Have you read Melville?" she said.

"*Moby-Dick.*"

This was only partly true. I had tried to read it, but only some of the chapters interested me. There were whole dense chapters of that book that when you tried to read them were like chewing on a brick. I knew I couldn't talk about Melville, or really about any of the books I had read. It was like sitting in front of a teacher who had all the answers while you had none of them. I lifted my napkin from my lap to my mouth; my cut thumb throbbed tightly with hot, methodic taps.

"And you must like Joyce," she said.

"Yes." I did like Joyce; I liked *Dubliners*.

She nodded, sipped.

But on the other hand, when I had to read *A Portrait of the Artist as a Young Man* for English class, I couldn't read it. I hated it. I didn't get what everybody at that dinner table was so mad about—priests, God, the government. I got so frustrated with that book that in a fit of disgust I swept it off my bed with a powerful backhand and it skittered across the floor and landed under my bureau, where it stayed for several weeks. I remembered the cover, reddish brown and yellow and a drawing of Joyce with his jutting chin and his googly little eyeglasses and his cursory mustache that didn't look right on his small face; it looked like a disguise.

I tried to think of something smart to say. "Joyce isn't . . . he's not American."

Hellman smiled. "No. He is not American."

"He's Irish."

Why did I say that? Everyone in the world knew he was Irish. It was about as useful as saying, "Sixty seconds make a minute."

"What grade are you in now?"

"Going into twelfth," I said.

She nodded. "You have brothers and sisters?"

"Yes."

"How old are they?"

Quickly, perhaps hoping that the numbers would sound different and fewer, I said, "Nineteen, twenty, twenty-one, twenty-two, twenty-three, twenty-four."

There was a silence while she calculated, and then her sparse eyebrows went up and she said, "My God," which was what people always said, and I knew they were thinking, *Hicks*. Barefoot Irish hicks who had no idea where the kids were coming from.

"And you're what? Seventeen?"

"My parents wanted us," I said. "It was all planned out." As soon as I said it I regretted it. I didn't have to defend them.

"What does your father do?"

She was looking at me steadily now, having finished her lunch. I couldn't tell whether she was truly curious or whether she was just being polite, whether she was talking to me because she was bored and there was nobody else to talk to. I had already told her my father was dead. She had forgotten. Now she was expecting to hear that he was a cop. I hated these questions.

"He's dead," I said. "He was a hematologist."

"When did he die?" she asked, without offering the usual apologetic pause or expression of sorrow.

"A long time ago."

"Why?" She reached for her cigarettes and plucked a paper match from a flattened Maison Robert matchbook. "Was he sick?"

The question was a surprise. People didn't usually ask that. Was he sick? I had to think about it. I remembered visiting him in a hospital with my mother, long, low buildings among some pines in winter, like a Boy Scout camp. There were patches of ice and snow on a thick bed of pine needles on either side of a paved path. I remembered my mother in her blue coat crutching carefully up the slippery hospital steps, her breath bursting white into the clear, cold air. We went down a hallway until we found my father's room. He was sitting in a chair and looked pale and strange, wearing pajamas in the middle of the day and his own maroon bathrobe from home. His hair, which he always wore in a crew cut, had grown a little longer. I wasn't used to seeing him like this. Why wasn't he dressed? He said, Hi, Rose, and asked me how old I was now, which was an odd thing for him to ask. He was my father. He should have known. He had been there a month, and during that time he had made a little wooden box with tiny brown and white tiles laid into its top in a pretty design. He had never done anything like that before. Nobody ever said anything about his heart or any other ailment. Nobody said anything about sickness at all. A few months later he died. He went to work one morning and didn't come home at night. By the time I went to bed that night he still wasn't home, and later, when I should have been asleep, I stood at the top of the stairs and saw nuns and police coming in our front door. The next morning in the kitchen my mother told us he was dead; he died of a heart attack at work. I went into the living room and looked out the window; I knew this meant he wouldn't be coming back. After that we hardly ever talked about it. It was a subject to be avoided. I didn't know why I wanted to avoid it, but it seemed to me that there was something wrong with it. And it made me strangely uncomfortable to talk about it now, as though a terribly bright light had been turned on me, its heat scalding my face and singeing my hair.

"He had a heart attack," I said.

Hellman lowered her hand from her mouth, and a cottony bulb of smoke tumbled voluptuously from between her parted lips, growing white and round as a golf ball; she snatched it back with a quick inhalation, and it disappeared down her throat. With her free hand she lifted the nearly bald ear of corn to her mouth, breathed smoke over it, then chewed it. "How old were you then?" she said through her teeth.

"Eight."

There was silence then, and she paused in her chewing with the cigarette in one hand and the corn held an inch before her mouth like a fat harmonica. She was suddenly preoccupied with some complex thought, her unblinking eyes dully searching the air above my head, the big, squarish lenses of her glasses reflecting the pale curve of my own forehead. Her fingers twitched as if enumerating. And then she lowered the corn and said with real interest, "How on earth did she manage?"

"Who?" I said, though I knew who.

"Your mother."

I never stopped to think about how my mother managed. Whenever I looked into the well of my own childhood, I saw first, for a brief moment, myself alone with my mother sitting on her bed in the silent house, and then in a burst of sound and color the surface of the water was broken and the rest of them appeared: twelve other eyes, twelve arms, twelve legs, six other mouths speaking in urgency or demand. Noise came from every corner of the house, hands banging on the piano, scraping at guitar strings, slamming a window shut, a muddy boot kicking a door, cries of delight or violence, a snowball ringing contemptuously against a window-pane, the stereo constantly clamoring with the sound of the Beatles, Bob Dylan, Joni Mitchell, the television spewing out the vaudeville sounds and sights of the Three Stooges for seven bodies stretched across my mother's bed like slaughtered soldiers stacked up at Antietam, staring dead-eyed. I saw my sisters Sheila and Elizabeth fighting upstairs every morning over some article of clothing. I saw Sheila, with three earrings in one earlobe and a lurid red lightbulb screwed into the lamp in her room, dancing atop her desk to the sound of the Kinks. I saw Stephen, Sheila, and Elizabeth crawling out a window onto the roof to smoke pot, Johnny shooting BB holes into a wall, Stephen hurling a dustpan through a plate-glass window, James banging the bathroom door open with a towel around his narrow waist and shouting, "Father stinkin' Lyons!" in frustration at some church-oriented question of my mother's, Ellen and myself jumping around the periphery of the living room without ever touching the floor, couch-to-table-to-radiator-to–love seat, knocking lamps as we went. I saw Johnny at the Milton Academy skating rink stealing cans of Tahitian Treat from the drink machine by snaking his skinny arm, in a Houdiniesque trick of contortion, up into its bowels, and Sheila so far ahead of the fashions that she caused a stir at her school when she showed up in army boots and a floppy hat and an old lady's dress, Elizabeth coming home in tears from the same school because Sheila had mocked her in front of her friends and then—causing yet another stir—had spat on a classroom wall. I heard James shouting, "Fuck yourself, you bitch," when my mother wouldn't let him buy a motorcycle. I saw the brilliantly lit Christmas tree in our living room tipping over with a crash, the bearded, long-haired boys Sheila once brought home to camp out on the living room floor, one of whom painted a fantastical green-and-red face on a wall upstairs. I saw, for that matter, the entire second floor of our house, which, because the stairs were difficult for her to climb, was just out of my mother's reach and thus had been allowed to flourish and grow wild, like a primeval forest: the floors littered with the play money of board games scattered like autumn leaves, chairs with broken legs, fat worms of compacted dust beneath the baseboards, dirty clothes flung across the floors like cumulus clouds across the sky, twisted apple cores rusting and curdling on the windowsills, Johnny in his new hockey skates, with their blades like two gleaming cleavers, traversing the playroom floor in stomping, hacking strides. I saw the scarred barn-wood playroom floor, with its skid marks and stains and copper-colored knots so perfectly round that I was endlessly tricked into thinking they were pennies, and the gaps between the boards wide enough to accommodate pistachio shells, quarters, screws, whole pencils. I saw the notes we left for each other in Magic Marker on the walls: *Baba sucks* and *Ellen, Marjery Albers caled and she wants you to call her back* and *Hi, Johnny, love me.* I saw the swastika that Johnny, enchanted with the ethos of *Hogan's Heroes,* had scratched into a windowpane when he was ten. I saw the two policemen who, with their bulk and swagger and smell of tobacco, were no less threatening to me than the robbers they had come to sniff out, poking through the upstairs rooms one summer night (we had arrived home from somewhere to discover that our house had been broken into) and confirming to each other with tremulous awe, "The bastards trashed the place." It was plain to all of us that not a single thing upstairs had been touched.

The tiny lines of age radiating from Hellman's lips were like basting stitches in a hem. She was looking at me, slightly slumped with her elbows on the table and her hands dangling beneath her chin and her eyes blinking patiently, like a drinker at ease at a bar, waiting for the end of the story. A drop of ash fell free from her cigarette onto her empty plate; too late she made a flicking gesture with her hand, an effort to claim responsibility for it. She wanted to know how my mother managed.

I heard my mother's bright voice ringing out in command: *clean up, put back, don't break, leave alone, eat all of, get off of, get out of, come home from, go down to, don't lie to, don't make a meal of, take your feet off of.* I saw her driving for the thousandth time down to Blanchard's liquor store and sending me or whichever one of my brothers and sisters was with her in for a fifth of Seagram's 7 and a pack of Lucky Strikes. I hated doing that; I knew what embarrassment and chaos and blank unavailability it would lead to. From time to time, in a rare and excruciating fit of frankness, I begged my mother not to drink, but she drank anyway. I hated those bottles, saw them as the cause of everything that was wrong with my life, but I went into the liquor store for her because she wanted me to; it was easier for me to hop out of the car and run in than it was for her to. When I refused to do it and sat stubbornly in my seat, it made her angry, caused her more trouble, and made me feel guilty and cruel. In the winter if I refused to do it, she might slip in the snow and get hurt. I didn't want to make things more difficult for my mother than they already were, but I despised this job, and as I walked up to the door of the liquor store I dragged my feet, like a person going to the gallows. Everything in that store was familiar: the fluorescent lights hanging from the ceiling, the skinny guy behind the counter in the cardigan and faded tie smoking a cigarette with a yellow pencil behind one ear and a ballpoint pen behind the other. He wore brown leisure slacks with a stretch waist and had a stubbly chin and a face gone gray with smoke and boredom. His hands trembled and his fingers were shiny-smooth and dirty from handling coins and bills. At nine, ten, and eleven I was still young enough to be surprised and enchanted by the store's automatic door, distracted for a moment from my odious task when the servile door with its gasping, sucking noise opened wide upon my approach. The place had the toasted dusty smell of the cardboard boxes stacked up in rows displaying their bottles. I didn't have to ask where the Seagram's was, I knew the aisle. The bottle was brown with a regally crowned red 7 on the front. I would put it down on the green Formica checkout counter, deliberately sliding it over the lesion of white scuffed into the counter's surface by years of bottles slid over it in just this way. Slim Jims and Beer Nuts hung in packages over the counter, and although I hadn't asked permission from my mother, I pulled down one or the other. I knew she wouldn't protest; Beer Nuts and Slim Jims were a payment for the services I had rendered: if she got what she wanted, I would get what I wanted. I asked the man for the cigarettes, and he dropped them on the counter saying, "How's Mum today?"

I always said, "Fine," and, with a flourish that was meant to be humorous, the man plucked the pen from behind his ear and handed it to me so I could fill in the amount on the check my mother had given me. I was careful to do it right. I didn't want to disappoint her. On the few occasions when she had forgotten to sign the check, I signed it for her in my juvenile script while the man smiled kindly on this triune of illegal activities. Nona R. Mahoney: it was swervy and swollen and looked nothing like her signature. "Tell Mum a big hello for me, will you?" the man would say, and I went out the door with the bottle under my arm, the cigarettes in one hand and the Beer Nuts in the other, tramping hatless across the brittle ice and snow toward my mother's car, a skinny, pale-faced girl with a part fashioned jaggedly down the middle of my scalp and a sky blue parka decorated with skiing penguins. As soon as we got home the bottle's pinkish paper seal would be broken.

Looking at Hellman's questioning face, I saw the Thanksgiving turkey falling from a platter in my mother's hands to the kitchen floor with a greasy, mushy thud. I saw five of us standing for hours in the cold outside the closed skating rink, waiting hopelessly for our mother to come and pick us up. I saw Baba and Ellen trying to maintain some modicum of order by cooking the dinner and telling me to set the table. I saw Ellen and myself taking the bottles and putting them upstairs where she couldn't get them, and then, guilty over the unfair advantage we had taken of her handicap, feeling too powerful and cruel, we brought them down again. I saw Ellen, fourteen and unlicensed, pulling up to the trolley station in my mother's car to pick me up when my mother was asleep on her bed and couldn't do it, Stephen fifteen and unlicensed driving us all home from some New Year's Eve party because she was drunk, and when the police stopped us he told them the truth; they took one look at her, and at the pale, frightened faces staring in the backseat of the car, and let us go. I saw Ellen and myself hiding in the woods by our school after the school fair, while people searched for us because our mother was asleep with her head on a table. I saw myself on long, late afternoons sitting stiffly in the sunlit kitchen so she couldn't begin drinking, while the shouts of kids playing in the field behind the house drifted through the windows. My watchful, prohibitive eyes, as she potted plants at the sink or did the laundry or prepared a stew, kept her from bringing down the bottle and pouring a drink until the arrival of a respectable hour. She wouldn't pour it in front of me. She had promised she wouldn't drink, but I knew she probably would if I left the room. She always did, filling a teacup with whiskey and hiding it in a cabinet, and so I sat there doing nothing, pretending that I wanted to be there. She knew, and I knew.

I saw myself in bare feet and a nightgown waiting endlessly at the dark living room window for my mother to come from somewhere, endlessly steering her to her bed, undressing her and pulling the blankets up over her shoulders, endlessly lying to people to protect her because I thought unhappiness was shameful. I saw myself hurling a whiskey bottle full force against an outcropping of bedrock beside our house, shattering it into amber slivers on the gray rock.

"She worked pretty hard, I guess." The words dropped like pebbles from my mouth. I knew that they were true, truer than I could explain to anyone who didn't know her. Her job was never over. In my discomfort I couldn't bring myself to say anything else.

"I should say so," Hellman said. "I should certainly say so. So many children to bring up alone. Brave woman. She must be very strong."

I lay my hands flat on the table. In their obvious sincerity her words glittered in the air before me like a small gift. Brave and strong. People had uttered the same words about my mother before, but this was different. If Lillian Hellman had spent thirty seconds thinking this about my mother, it was nearly as good as having her think it about me.

"She is," I said and I knew this, too, was true.

The wind lurched, and a fistful of rain clacked against the

kitchen window. "Yes." She nodded, and then as she crushed out her cigarette the very atmosphere seemed to tighten around her again, taking on its usual inviolable indifference, and I knew that her eyes had stopped seeing me, turning instead to the next thing in her mind. I knew our lunch was over, that the level platform we had been sitting on was tilting now to tip me back into my place. She got up out of her chair and headed for the sink, and, as though she had forgotten that this was my day off, she asked me to clear the table.

FROM *Chasing Grace: Reflections of a Catholic Girl, Grown Up*

MARTHA MANNING

GOLDFISH

I AM BY PROFESSION a psychologist. One might assume that this enhances my ability as a mother. It does not. In fact, it is more often an impediment than an aid. My assumption is that exploring feelings and sharing those feelings with loved ones is the way to live an enlightened life. But things get complicated when one's child does not share this conviction—and from birth wages active resistance against it.

I should have known it with the goldfish when she was just four years old. All the signs were there. Her goldfish, Harvard and San Diego, were, as she often lamented, "the closest I'll ever get to having pets." Keara was a mastermind at guilt and it was never wasted on her mother, who was allergic to all fur-bearing animals.

At the pet store, she stood for an eternity surveying the goldfish, offering personality analyses of each. The fish all looked the same to me, but not to her. "She looks like a brat." "This one's too shy." She finally picked the two she determined had the most lively "personalities." But it didn't end there. The goldfish trade had become considerably more complicated than when I was a child. In addition to the necessities of a bowl and a net, there were special fish-food flakes, dechlorination drops, algae, special rocks, and even fish toys. I assented to everything but the fish toys until Keara delivered the zinger, "Mom, they'll get lonely too while you're out working." More guilt. It worked. The fish got their toys.

Harvard and San Diego moved into her room with great ceremony and excitement. But after less than thirty minutes of intent goldfish watching, she didn't find them all that interesting. In fact, by the end of the day, I wished we had just rented them, like videos that can only be kept overnight.

Instead of teaching my child to be responsible, having goldfish taught me how to be responsible for my child. Initially, I was quite diligent in caring for her pets, or as she continued to call them, her "almost pets." But after a while, even I became lax. Sitting at dinner, I'd get a twinge and ask urgently, "Has anyone fed the goldfish lately?" With that, one of us would gasp, run upstairs, and give them a sprinkle of fish-food flakes.

Their bowl became grungier with time, with my husband and I waging silent standoffs about whose turn it was to clean it. When Keara's room began to smell like a swamp, one of us broke down and lugged the bowl to the kitchen sink, all the while lamenting the general lack of responsibility in our household. Then came the weekly disagreement about whose idea it was to get the "damn goldfish," as they were affectionately called, in the first place.

Somehow Keara always managed to extricate herself from the whole mess, quite content to let her father and me battle it out.

I'll never forget that day. "D-Day," my husband calls it. It was Thanksgiving. The kind of cold, dark, New England day that helps you understand why the pilgrims almost didn't make it. We were expected at relatives' in the early afternoon and spent the morning catching up with the week's dirty rooms, dishes, and laundry. When I came close to Keara's room, the smell and the crud on the bowl told me there was no escaping it—the bowl had to be cleaned. But I was distracted. It had been a tough week—too much work, difficult patients. But I'm making excuses again. After all these years, I still feel bad about what I did. This guilt is reinforced constantly by a family that won't let me forget.

Things started out well. I scrubbed the bowl and changed the water. It sounds easy, but it isn't. Those little fish were always tough to get back into their bowl. One of them usually ended up flipping out of the net and panicking on the kitchen floor. And goldfish aren't easy to retrieve when they're upset. In retrospect, they actually had some cause for concern. As I scooped San Diego off the floor, I tried to reassure him in my best psychologist's voice, which had about as much impact on the fish as it ever did on my child.

We were doing fine until we got to the dechlorinating part. Anyone who's owned goldfish knows that tap water is not good for them and that several drops of chemicals must be added to rid the water of chlorine. Unfortunately, this proved to be one of those cases in which there actually can be too much of a good thing.

The phone rang as I was placing the drops in the bowl, and from what we could piece together later, I must have put a couple too many drops in. I scooped the fish back into the bowl and continued to talk on the phone. In no more than five seconds, they shot to the top of the bowl, turned side up, and floated rigidly in their extraordinarily clean water.

"Oh no! The goldfish! I have to hang up!"

I yelled for my husband to come quickly.

I pointed to the bowl.

"What did you do to the goldfish?"

"I don't know," I answered. "Do you think they're dead?"

"No, I think they're doing the sidestroke. Of course they're dead. How did you do that?"

"Would you keep your voice down?" I hissed between clenched teeth. "I don't know; maybe I put too many drops in. Anyway, it was *your* turn," I said, trying to share the burden of guilt. "How are we going to tell her?"

"What do you mean, we? You did it. You tell her."

She was watching *Sesame Street*, sitting cross-legged on the family-room couch.

"Hi, Sweetie. I have some bad news . . . Harvard and San Diego aren't alive anymore."

"You mean they're dead?"

"Well, yeah, pretty much." I was having a hard time being direct. Her trusting blue eyes had filled with enormous tears that were beginning a torturously slow descent down her cheeks.

"Something happened while I was cleaning their bowl, maybe too many drops. You see too many chemicals can . . ." I hoped a scientific explanation might gain us some distance from the pain.

"Oh no," she wailed. "I'll miss them so much."

"Honey, would you please stop saying that. I'll get you more tomorrow. First thing. I promise."

She put her head down against the couch and started to cry.

"Keara, is there anything I can do for you?" I whispered as I put my arm around her.

"Yeah," she sniffed. "Leave me alone."

I can't remember too many times when I've felt like a worse mother. Not only was I the perpetrator of my child's pain, I was totally inept in comforting her about it.

What could I do with all this distress? I searched for ways to salvage the unfortunate situation. Then it came to me. This was actually a golden moment, an opportunity to teach one of life's great lessons, to share something of great significance with my child. I would transform this awful mistake into something good. We would have a funeral. A goldfish funeral for the dearly departed Harvard and San Diego. My husband suggested a "burial at sea": a couple of kind words, a flush, and that would be that. I could not believe his callousness. Plus, I reasoned, flushing dead things would be confusing to a child of this age.

It was time to teach her about death, about the observance of loss, and about getting on with life. I began to get really enthusiastic about the funeral idea. I figured we could obtain a lot of mileage out of these goldfish. I began to feel less helpless, even optimistic that I could convert this random accident into an important family milestone.

I quickly prepared the service in my head. We would each say a few words about the fish and bury them under the deck in the backyard. I found a small plastic bag and scooped the fish out of the bowl. My garden tools were packed away for the winter, so I grabbed an old fork to use for digging the hole. I called everyone to come outside.

That was when the trouble started.

Keara yelled down, "Oh, Mom, it's too cold and *Sesame Street* isn't over yet."

My husband echoed her resistance, warning, "You do remember, don't you, that we are expected at dinner in an hour."

I was undaunted. "Come on. This will only take a minute. It's important."

We pulled on our coats and went to the backyard. It had begun to sleet, and even I found it terribly cold. I carried the bag with reverence and ceremony. Solemnly, I asked my daughter to choose a spot. She pointed halfheartedly to a spot on the ground and added, "This is really gross."

We stood silently for a moment. Then I asked her if she'd like to say any final words. She looked down for a moment, so I assumed she was collecting her thoughts. I was ready to be moved. Then she shrugged casually and said, "No, not really."

"Well, can't you think of *something*?" I prompted.

"Like what?"

"Like how they were good goldfish. Like how you liked having them in your room. Like how you'll miss them."

"Yeah, Mom. That's good."

"No, honey, they were *your* goldfish. I thought you might want to say something in your own words." I was beginning to grit my teeth, and the tone of my voice sounded more like a command than a suggestion. "What would *you* like to say?"

"What I would like to say is, Mom, how much longer is this going to take?"

My husband pointed to the sleet and remarked again about the time and the cold.

At that point I could have easily added them to the day's killing spree.

"Listen, we're going to bury these damn goldfish, so you might as well participate." I bent down and struck the rocky soil with my little fork. It was New England November frozen solid. I tried again . . . and again. The fork was no match for the ground and began to bend. A couple of bits of dirt loosened. I struck harder. Even in the cold, I was working up a sweat. I looked up from my crouch to see my husband and daughter staring at me as if I were an alien. This made me angrier, and I stabbed the ground even harder. Every few stabs, I laid the little bag in the indentation of earth I'd made to see if it was deep enough.

Keara piped up, "Mom, you're going to have to go much deeper than that."

"Did it ever occur to the two of you that you might help?"

"But there's only one fork," they replied lamely.

I loosened more dirt and ground the bag into what could only optimistically be called a hole. Then I collected rocks to cover what the dirt didn't. I stood up holding my battered fork and began the service. "Everything has a beginning and an end. Some things live a very long time. And other things live a very short time. This is what life is all about. *It's nobody fault.* Sometimes life . . ."

"Mom," Keara cut me short, "I'm shivering. Can I please go in?"

"Yes, go in. Go ahead, both of you. Go in and ruin this whole thing," I whined in my best martyr voice, which was totally wasted on them. They were halfway to the house when, over her shoulder, Keara finally offered her send-off to the deceased, "Bye, guys." That was as close to a benediction as the child was going to get.

I stood alone, in the cold, with the buried fish. Little pieces of bag stuck out from the rocks and the dirt. But it was getting late.

This clearly had not gone the way I had hoped. I needed to cut my losses and bring the ceremony to a close.

"Well, guys, I'm really sorry it came to this. You know I didn't mean it."

I was talking to dead goldfish, half hoping one would offer absolution from the grave. Slowly it became evident to me that this was just another mistake I would have to tolerate. I gave a heavy sigh and walked into the house, thinking about how things always worked out better in the movies or on television or in other people's families.

We brought more goldfish. This time it took only two minutes to pick them out.

She didn't give a thought to the names. She just called them Harvard and San Diego again. They took up residence in her room, and she seemed to adjust to the loss quite well. It took some time for me to recover from a serious case of bowl-cleaning phobia, especially with my husband and daughter joining in with the theme song from the movie *Jaws*, with one of them always leering, "Just when you thought it was safe to be a goldfish . . ." Within two weeks, I recovered my sense of humor and felt renewed confidence in my capacity to care for fish.

Several weeks later, I went to pick up Keara from her preschool. As I climbed the stairs, I noticed signs announcing "Dr. Martha Manning's talk on children's social development," a presentation I had agreed to months before that was scheduled for later in the week. Lining the hall walls were brand-new projects the children had done on the theme "Feelings."

The title of these paintings was "The Saddest Thing . . ." I was touched by the children's paintings, already calculating how I could integrate them into my talk that week. Then I stopped in horror at Keara's. Despite her rudimentary drawing skills, the picture was unmistakable. Two dead goldfish floated at the top of a bowl of water. Above her picture were Keara's words, dictated to a teacher and printed in big, bold, black letters:

THE SADDEST THING . . . WAS WHEN MY MOM KILLED MY GOLD-FISH!

Her name was written under it in huge letters. Two horrible scenes immediately flashed in front of me. The first was the picture of Dr. Martha "Bad Mother" Manning addressing the parents of the preschoolers later that week. The second scenario involved Keara, sometime in the future, on a therapist's couch working through her hostility at her fish-murdering mother.

Bad-mother mistakes never die. They take on a life of their own. They will never be forgotten. Bad-mother mistakes are inevitable. And the scary part is that I am making some now, probably at this very moment, without even knowing it. But she will know. And someday she will tell her friends or perfect strangers, or maybe even me in an angry moment. And I will be as puzzled as my mother looks each time I say accusingly, "Remember the time you . . ."

So in the meantime, I just do the best I can. I feed the fish when I remember. I clean the bowl when it can't be avoided. And no matter what else, I always count the dechlorination drops.

LAST WILL AND TESTAMENT

UPON MY IMPENDING DEATH, please read the following and comply as fully as possible.

Dying is bad enough. The combination of death and pain is unacceptable. Force the doctors to give me as many painkillers as it takes. Given the addictive branches of my family tree, I have heretofore been vigilant about avoiding dependence on drugs. But if I'm already dying, screw it. I want drugs—lots of them. Score them on the street if you have to.

Immediately post mortem, my husband (or closest living friend) is to empty my bedside drawer of the two vibrators, three Anaïs Nin books, and twelve sets of rosary beads. No one would understand.

I want a simple wake. Most people say they want to be buried in a plain wooden box. But somehow, when their families are vulnerable in loss, the death merchants make them feel cheap if they don't buy mahogany and brass, guaranteed waterproof. I mean it: I want a plain wooden box, like those the monks use to bury their brothers. Use the money you saved on a totally impractical car. Landscape the house with gorgeous flowers. Give the money to a poor man on the street. Whatever you choose, I promise that you'll get a lot more mileage out of it than I'll get out of a casket.

Don't let them put makeup on me and do weird stuff to my hair. Let me look as shitty as I did when I died. It will help people believe that I'm better off dead.

Don't dress me up. I'm going to have to spend a long time in those clothes. I recommend my navy sweatpants with my hooded gray sweatshirt, or my plaid flannel nightgown.

If anyone says, "She looks like she's sleeping," eject him or her forcefully from the room.

Do not allow carnations or gladioli anywhere near me.

At my wake, play the music I've always loved in the background. No "easy listening," which is just a euphemism for elevator music. Music shouldn't be easy. Just because I'm knocked out doesn't mean everyone else has to be. You can't go wrong with Motown, Puccini, or any woman with the earth in her voice. For my funeral I would like the Magnificat (in Latin), "I Don't Feel No Ways Tired," and "Precious Lord."

Don't mourn me politely. Make a huge scene. You'll feel better.

Don't leave me alone in the funeral home. I get frightened around dead people.

My daughter is to receive all my published and unpublished writing. I have separated the unpublished manuscripts and journals into specific decades or events in her life. I have reserved writing for her forties that she couldn't possibly appreciate in her twenties. There is a collection for when she gets married, for when she becomes a mother, for when she begins to lose heart, for her great successes, for her lowest moments. I will leave it to her to decide the appropriate time to open each box. I would ask that she be gentle with me as she reads the words I have left behind. They were never meant as words of wisdom, only as markers of my particular journeys.

The following document is to be given to my daughter upon my death.

As you know, the women in my family live to be very old and fairly cranky, which your father always said was fine, since the men in his family tend to die young. I know that he will leave you his own advice. As the firstborn girl, of a firstborn girl, of a firstborn girl, of a firstborn girl, of a firstborn girl, of a firstborn girl, I know you already have the strength that comes from that kind of matriarchal lineage. Here are some words of wisdom from your great-great-grandmother, your great-grandmother, your grandmother, and me.

GREAT-GREAT-GRANDMOTHER (GRAMMIE HALE)

DON'T BITE YOUR NAILS. Nails go directly to the heart, and when you die and the doctors examine your heart, it will be all punctured with nails. [Good advice, bad reason.]

Always own a home with a hole in the center. Do no housework, just push everything down the hole, so you can spend your time doing creative things. [Good idea, but I was never able to find the hole.]

Don't tell anyone your "business." If you don't want it as tomorrow's headline, keep it to yourself. Don't tell "family tales." [No comment, for obvious reasons.]

Don't look at strangers, talk to them, or go with them. They will take you to a forest with a warren of underground tunnels—filled with kidnapped children—and do Bad Things [never elaborated] to you.

Be vigilant about your bowel movements. Check them for signs of bad color or content, and report them immediately. [She never said to whom.]

Never go on amusement-park rides. Your insides will get scrambled and they will never return to the right place. [What can I say?]

Don't put anything in your mouth that you picked up from the ground. Remember the boy who ate a piece of popcorn from the ground that an octopus had crawled into. And the octopus grew and grew inside his stomach until one day it exploded and the boy died. [Form your own conclusion.]

GREAT-GRANDMOTHER (GRANDMOTHER COONEY)

DON'T EVER GET MORE education than your husband. It will ruin your marriage. [Disregard.]

There is nothing more important than family. [Have it tattooed on your hand.]

The beach is the best place for healing—hydrotherapy and heliotherapy can get anyone back on track. [I totally agree.]

Monitor your soul and your bowels closely. Saturday evening is a good time for a complete cleaning: confession, a bath, and an enema—whether you need it or not. [I will leave this for your own interpretation.]

GRANDMOTHER (GRANDMOTHER MANNING)

BOYS ARE LIKE STREETCARS—one comes along every few minutes. [Which, in the recounting from me to Sarah to Priscilla, became, "Boys are like streetcars. You get off one, you get on another." Feel free to chose either the Thomas Wolfe version or the Aunt Priscilla version.]

Always keep the kitchen clean. The rest of the house can go to hell, but if the kitchen is clean, you can cope. [True.]

On suffering: Offer it up for the souls in Purgatory. [Someone might as well get something out of it.]

No one can embarrass you but yourself. [Good advice—and the possibilities are endless.]

If you can't say something nice, don't say anything at all. [Nice sentiment, but then there is 50 percent less to say.]

Don't get weighed more than once a year. [Is that possible?]

Pay as little attention to your bowels as your health will allow. [Thank God.]

When people say, "How are you?" remember that they are not looking for a health report. [True.]

Life's not fair. Get used to it. [Correct, but try to find a gentler way to say it.]

Put ice on it. [Depends where.]

MY ADVICE

ALWAYS BE SUSPICIOUS OF a person, a restaurant, or a hotel that describes itself with *clean* as the first adjective. If that is its best quality, I have serious reservations about the honesty or relevance of anything else on the list.

Economy is another terrible word. *Cheap* is better. Economy implies that you're getting a good deal. Cheap says it's inexpensive and makes absolutely no promises about quality.

Avoid anything that advertises itself as "family style." Family style is a euphemism for chaos and includes all kinds of behaviors that I hope you will never tolerate in your own family. The bad news is that the food is always overcooked to the point of tastelessness. The good news is that you can have as much as you want. Family-style places allow you to compare your family against other people's—children running around like wild animals letting out fork-dropping, glass-breaking, mind-curdling screams, and older couples staring vacantly past each other as they eat like robots and wonder if they are having a good time.

If you insist on continuing to be a vegetarian, take vitamins.

I'm with my mother on the bowel thing.

Read a lot. Anything you can get your hands on. Roll around in language.

Delight in words. Know the challenge of finding the exact, best, perfect word to define your experience.

Let music continue to be your constant companion. Don't let your tastes fossilize. Try the new stuff. Dance whenever you can.

Learn to cook. I'm sorry I never taught you. Hopefully you've picked up something from your father.

Continue the rituals of our family. Add to them. Light the candles every Sunday evening in Advent. Fill the living room with at least fifty candles on Christmas Eve. Light every one of them. Allow everybody to open one gift. Appreciate the light as it flickers across the faces of the people you love. Write out elaborate rhyming clues for Easter egg hunts. On July 4, continue with the only baking I ever taught you—our annual flag cake. If you feel especially energetic, make another one like we used to on July 14, and try to sing "La Marseillaise" the whole way through. Use real whipped cream, raspberries, and blueberries. On Thanksgiving morning, contribute to the feeding of someone else. When you leave your children for trips, give them something they can open every night or morning. A letter, a lollipop—some concrete thing that lets them know you are thinking of them.

Celebrate each transition fully—birthdays, graduations, anniversaries, accomplishments. Observe loss and the memory of that loss over time. Do it enough the same way each year to give you a sense of tradition, and throw in something new to add your own imprint. Rituals are the punctuation marks in our lives. Don't get sloppy with them. Sometimes they are the only anchor in a life that feels adrift.

Cherish your friends. This will be more important for you than for many people. Because you are an only child, you will have to work harder at preserving a sense of family than I did. Remember that you can have family in any loving, cohesive group, even when no one is related by blood.

Even though it requires effort, stay in touch with your aunts, uncles, and cousins. A family helps you to remember who you are and what you come from. You know well the problems our family has faced. But you also know the wonders. Remember that you can have a great family no matter how many of its members are wrestling demons. In a family, the whole is always greater than the sum of its parts. The synergistic energy created in a good family is nourishment for a lifetime.

Love like crazy. When you're ready, commit yourself to someone entirely. Expect rough patches, and then expect boring patches that make the rough ones look good. Remember that love in a relationship changes, the same way that a person's face changes over time. But with care, the essence can remain intact. I remember lines from a poem by William Carlos Williams about his marriage: "We have survived to keep the jeweled prize always at our fingertips. We will it so and so it is. Past all accident." I believe that it takes more than sheer will to make a relationship work, but those lines have reminded me on numerous occasions not to let love slip too far away.

If it's possible, have a child. I hope you find a partner with whom to share your life. But don't wait too long for the child. My most impulsive and best decision was to have you when I was young and stupid, studying like hell to be smart on no money and a lot of hope. When I became smart, and reason took over, I planned my life, inserting the idea of more children at point A and then point B. As you know, it didn't work out.

If you have a child, give yourself generously to her childhood. Not just an hour in the evening after work, or on weekends. Break the rules about who should do what. But don't sacrifice the child in the name of anything. Remember Uncle Darrell and Uncle Greg, who stayed home with Chelsea and Tori while their mothers continued with their careers. Remember Aunt Ann, who stayed home while Uncle Chip worked, and loved it so much that she was unhappy when she needed to return to work. Remember Dad, re-arranging his schedule for every field hockey game, for school trips. Expect a man to share fully in the nourishment of a child. Demand it of yourself as well. If it means that your careers coast for a while, let them coast. If it means making do on less money, make do. Don't accept anyone's bullshit that "working mothers" are respon-sible for the breakup of the family. Everyone is responsible for the family. But also don't delude yourself about the needs of children. They need a lot. Sometimes, more than you think you have in you. I'm not just saying this for the benefit of your child. I'm saying that you should do it, also, for yourself. Being a mother is the best thing I've ever done with my life. But a number of years passed, when I was struggling with other things, before I realized that.

Find work that you love—even if it's not the work you're get-ting paid for. Make sure there's always a fire burning someplace in your life. It makes the rest of it bearable. Take chances. Screw up. Don't be polite. It's a total waste of time.

Ask for help when you need it. Know that it is a sign of char-acter and not, as I used to think, a lack of it.

Find a spiritual home. I don't care what religion it is. But give yourself to some belief, to some sense of worship, for awe of that which is beyond you. Read the writings of the many holy women and men through the ages. Their words can infuse your life with direction and purpose. Pray. Work for justice and peace. Know your own strength. Don't let the gravity of the status quo paralyze you and make you complacent. Allow a place in your life for righteous anger.

Don't get too attached to stuff. Everything around you will tell you the opposite. But remember the first time I went to that ritzy shopping mall after those horrible years of depression, ending with the hospital and ECT. Remember how I said that I felt like a Martian and everything looked crazy to me? Well, it wasn't just because I was crazy. You and Dad blanched when I said I wanted to stand up on a chair and yell, "You people . . . go home . . . what you're looking for . . . I swear, it's not here!" But that was actually one of the sanest moments of my life. Take pleasure in the things you have. But always ask yourself whether the thing you're dying for at the moment is something you *want* or something you *need*. Wanting is okay; just don't let it masquerade as needing. It screws up your decisions. If you go offtrack on this, just drive slowly through the poorest part of the city, or take a working trip to a third-world country. Look for women your age. Look for children. Think again about the difference between your need and theirs, between your want and theirs.

Get comfortable with your body. Treat it well. Put it to work. Give it rest. Let yourself love the way you look. I can't give you any more advice on that. I never got that far.

Make friends with silence. Know the grace of your own company, and I promise, you will never be alone.

from *Monkeys*

Susan Minot

Wildflowers

"Maybe we should help her," said Sophie, sitting on the window seat of the front room. The open windows let in the luffing of sails and the clanging of halyards, but louder than that were dishes, making a clatter in the kitchen.

"She hasn't asked," said Caitlin with a smile. Their feet, barely touching, did not move. Out in the harbor sailboats were circling one another, tacking this way and that, positioning themselves before the starting gun. Kids in rowboats shot jackknife sprays with their oars while other kids watched from railings above. Mum passed by the living room and out the door. Sophie and Caitlin heard her squeal in the wind and rolled their eyes. She reappeared on the dock carrying a plate of brownies in one hand and a vase of flowers in the other. Her dress fluttered about her, the vase bent back like a torch. It was part of it for the ladies giving the Saturday race teas to bring flowers, usually from their own gardens—careful arrangements of dahlias and zinnias and sweet william. Mum had brought wildflowers—loosestrife and buttercups and queen anne's lace. There was no space for a garden at the Vincents', with the dock in front and Main Street just up the steps—the vegetable garden was in another place entirely—so Mum gathered flowers up island. She found fields everywhere shimmering down to the sea, flowers scattered and random, not boxed inside walls. On her bedside table she kept a small vase, always fresh.

"She's feeling her oats," Sophie said, watching Mum head for the clubhouse at the end of the dock. Inside the mahogany darkness, other bright dresses were crossing back and forth.

"She thinks she needs to say hello to everyone in sight," said Caitlin.

Upstairs along the hall a series of doors slammed in the draft, one after another.

"Guess-Who must be racing today," said Sophie.

Caitlin, studying the scene, nodded.

THE CROWD THAT SHOWED up two hours later at the clubhouse was not large but it was dense. Everyone clustered together; they'd known each other a long time. Beneath the pyramid of yachting flags were familiar tennis hats and faded salmon shorts, warped Top-Siders and yellowing socks. Short, lime-green skirts, fashionable anywhere else in 1970, were here on North Eden nothing new. They were what the ladies wore and always had worn playing golf.

Apart from the crowd, slumped against the tackle shed, were

the wayward teenagers in torn blue jeans and Indian prints. Caitlin and Sophie, among them, snuck drags from a furtive cigarette. Mum was sitting near the clubhouse doorway in front of a silver samovar, handing cups of tea upward with napkins pressed beneath. Chicky, the youngest Vincent, was waiting near her elbow for a cookie. According to their grandmother, Chicky looked exactly like Dad. She had said the same thing about each baby, as Mum had had them, seven of them one right after another. Caitlin and Sophie, the first babies, had been dressed in blue for the first years of their lives, in honor of the Blessed Virgin. Mum had been taught by nuns. After her seventh baby, she stopped listening to the pope. She was thirty-nine years old now, her last baby, Chicky, was six, and for the first time since marrying Dad, she had no little fists clutching at her hem, the way they would in department stores. "Hold on," she'd say before weaving off through crowded aisles.

"Just one," she whispered to Chicky. He snuck a cookie from a china plate. Around the corner kids were lined up for ice cream being scooped out of a cardboard tub by freckled Amy Haffenreffer, who preferred the company of children. Out on the thorofare by the spindle, the last of the sailboats were tacking in to the finish line, each at a different angle, all at a heel.

Caitlin nudged Sophie. Mum was pouring a cup of tea. The man next to her had a grayish white spot on the back of his dark head, and Mum's eyes were lit with a brightness. When her sister Grace visited, sitting on the porch in her smart wool dresses and silk kerchiefs and black sunglasses, telling New York stories, Mum would get that look, giggling now and then in an odd, excited way. The first time the girls had seen it had been years ago in the lamplight, when they'd all spent the night in the cabin on Boxed Island.

Mum came flying out of the cricket darkness, her nightgown luminous, a fiery look in her eye. She was panting. On her way to the outhouse, she'd seen a fox, a silver fox. "It streaked across my path," she said. Her hands trembled and toyed with the ruffle at her neck; her pupils were lit in bright points from the oil lamp.

"No such thing," said Dad, thumping at a flimsy mattress.

Mum stood there transfixed. She turned to her babies, all six of them in diminishing sizes, rolled up in flannel sleeping bags. "As silver as the Silver Orient," she said. It was from a story they all knew, one Mum had read to them, about the train that took off from its tracks and flew over the Alps.

Later when the cabin was dark, Caitlin and Sophie heard Mum and Dad mumbling across the room. "Oh they'll forget about it by tomorrow," Mum said. But they didn't. It was one of those things they remembered and mentioned now and then, about that time the silver fox streaked across Mum's path and how her eyes were lit, not with fright, and how Dad said there was no such thing.

When Mum handed the man a cup of tea, the look was there: thrilled. Wilbur Kittredge had his collar turned up against his tanned skin. He was the head of a large international company. He made bombs.

The Kittredge estate was set high on a bluff of North Eden. The main house had a long porch that overlooked the bay where humped islands scattered off into tiny dots. The estate had stables and an electric fence and guest cottages and a walled-in garden where stone satyrs huddled, ears pointed, fingers secretly at their lips. They had exotic animals, antelopes and a snow leopard and crocodiles, and special guests. A Balinese fire dancer had performed under the moon; an American Indian had constructed an authentic teepee. The topiary garden was designed by an Italian monk to depict a tennis match. A man sculpted in privet served a green ball to a sculpted woman in a flared privet skirt crouched at a slender privet hedge. Each year the Kittredges had a clambake and invited the whole island—all the summer people, that is, and certain islanders who knew who they were. But the main attraction was the carriages. Wilbur Kittredge had over forty antique carriages lined up in a special barn. There were scenes painted on the shiny doors, polished brass railings, leather seats and velvet seats and fringed surreys with wicker sides. When Dad was home in Marshport during the week, Mum went on rides.

Wilbur Kittredge was a special friend of Mum's. Over the years, he'd sent her presents, strange items from strange lands. One package held an odd wreath of shellacked flowers, which Mum hung over the mitten basket. Caitlin and Sophie knew that if Dad had given her something like that it would have gone straight to the cellar. Some things just weren't Mum's taste. When his first son, Gus, was born, after three girls, Dad brought Mum gladiolas. To make it worse, they were yellow. His presents made Mum bite her lip; there was a whole world of things "not me" or "a little off." Dad learned to leave the sales slip in the box.

THE TEENAGERS WERE DISCUSSING various figures in the crowd. "Ol' Will Kittredge is looking pretty dapper," said Westy Granger sullenly.

"Is your father up?" asked Trisha Holt, who had painted a rose on her cheek.

Everyone on the island minded each other's business. You always knew who was up or not. Everyone knew that Wilbur Kittredge's wife was at a spa in California.

"He got up yesterday," Sophie said. "He's probably at the garden." The vegetable garden was in the middle of the island on a bit of land their grandfather had bought long ago. The garden was one of Dad's projects. He'd grown the plants from seed in soil cubes that sat on a green plastic tray in the laundry room. He studied each seed as if it were a jewel, releasing it and brushing the dirt over with his baby finger. Each night he brought back something for supper: small clubs of zucchini, ripe tomatoes, string beans with their raw fiber-glass skin, and carrots luminous under creases of dirt.

Dad had other projects. For after-dinner, he liked to carve small birds. He was rebuilding the back walkway. There were mooring lines to be spliced onto buoys. When they were little, Dad built a lot of things, a bicycle hutch, a playhouse down in the woods, a treehouse with three separate platforms. Whenever a new baby came home, he'd built something for it. He constructed a bassinet with a step around it so the girls could stand and watch while Mum gave the baby a bath. They watched her fold the diapers fiercely, her eyes with an intent glare, clenching pins in her teeth, pins with plastic tulips on them.

To Caitlin and Sophie it seemed there always was a new baby. When it came home from the hospital, Caitlin and Sophie dressed up as Indians and made cards for Mum. The bundle got picked up and put down, and when it was left in its carriage, it lifted its head to stare at the back. Caitlin and Sophie looked into the black carriage at the baby's head bobbing around like a buoy, staring at nothing. It could stare at nothing for hours.

It was in the baby carriage that Frances died. She was the fifth baby. Only Caitlin and Sophie could remember it, being six and five. It was in the afternoon. Mum came home with shopping bags crinkling, wearing her Boston suit and with her hair in a puff from the hairdresser's. Delilah and Gus were there—everyone always came running into the hall when Mum came home. She picked Baby Frances out of the carriage where it was parked on the porch. Mum went tucking at the baby's throat. Suddenly she was in a hurry, pulling the baby tight to her, touching the baby's face. The kids all looked. Mum spat out, "Get down in the playroom," more mean than she'd ever yelled before. They weren't important anymore at all. Mum ran into the TV room and Caitlin saw her put her mouth on top of Baby Frances's mouth, trying to dial the phone at the same time. Then she slammed it down and went tearing out the hall and down the steps and onto the driveway toward the Birches'.

The next day and for a while after the driveway was filled with cars and the house with people. Caitlin and Sophie found ashtrays next to their toothbrushes in the bathroom and teacups on the piano bench. Baby Frances, they were told, was now in heaven and the grown-ups looked down at them as if they didn't understand. There were flowers everywhere, baskets on tables, pots on the floor, carefully shaped pyramids or clipped round globes.

One day, Sophie saw Mum sitting alone in the living room, where no one ever was, on the arm of a chair in a slouch. Her thumb moved slowly up and down her elbow, smoothing it over.

Downstairs in the playroom Caitlin said it was because Mum still missed Baby Frances. Sophie said she did too.

"Well," Delilah said, "I'm not going to die."

"You have to," Caitlin said. "Everyone in the world has to."

"Not me," Delilah said, pressing her eyelashes down. "I'm going to be the first one in the world not to."

"But that's impossible, Delilah."

"Just wait."

They were all drawing pictures of the family, cards to give Mum and Dad. You lined everyone up according to age. In the sky they put an angel with a halo and wings and black hair for Baby Frances.

The next baby, Sherman, came less than a year after. He was a bad crier. He had a long high screech that would suddenly stop as if a switch had been thrown. After a long silence he'd launch again into even higher wails, gasps to make up for the time spent not breathing.

AMONG THE TEA DRINKERS on the wharf was a trio of strangers to North Eden, two swarthy men and a statuesque blond woman near the sail closet. They looked European.

"Kittredge houseguests," said Westy Granger.

"I bet they're folksingers," said Trisha Holt. "They look like Peter, Paul, and Mary."

"More like a Swedish movie star," said Westy's friend with the long hair. "Quite a T-shirt on her."

"The mystery woman perhaps," said Westy.

The other night they were careening home from a moonless party at Blind Man's Beach when they came upon a dark carriage clip-clopping along the Middle Road. Red lamps were swinging from points up front and there were two silhouettes under the fringed awning. The car slowed down and pulled to the side and everyone looked. Next to Mr. Kittredge was a woman with a hat on. Caitlin dug her elbow into Sophie's rib. A thin fly whip passed across the rosy lights, waving them on. Westy screeched forward and began to sing the chorus of an antiwar song and everyone joined in.

The fact that Mr. Kittredge made bombs did not, according to Mum, mean that he was bad. She recognized the bad guys. She threw her shoe at Nixon when he was on TV. She distributed leaflets after the bombing of Cambodia and gave cocktail parties with Patricia Meyer, the only other Democrat in Marshport, to raise money for their candidates. Years before, on a tour of the Capitol, they visited their senator and afterward Mum brought Caitlin and Sophie to visit Mr. Kittredge. Mum liked to look at other people's houses. While she was touring the greenhouse and the collection rooms and the new addition, Caitlin and Sophie swam in the Kittredges' slate pool without anyone watching, something they'd never done before. None of the other Kittredges were there but they never were. The afternoon air was hushed, with only heat bugs going, and when it started to rain, the girls slipped into the pool house. It had an automatic ice maker and ceramic elephants under glass tabletops, cushions trimmed in green bamboo patterns, and a pair of tusks taller than the girls, guarding the doorway. Silver frames showed the blond Kittredge daughters in bathing suits, waist-deep in turquoise water, glinting gold jewelry. When Mum and Mr. Kittredge got back, he lifted a trapdoor and led them down cement steps into a cement room, the bomb shelter. In the corner were boxes of dried food stacked up like bricks. Of all the things she saw, Mum said, the glass orchids were her favorite. Mum always told the girls her favorite things.

WILBUR KITTREDGE POKED HIS head out of the clubhouse door and waved to the two men and the blond woman. They appeared amused with their surroundings, observing the scene with an air of irony. Wilbur Kittredge seemed to share their private joke and greeted them warmly when they joined him. Mum turned in her seat to be introduced, her shoulders stiff, her smile polite, and her eyes lightning-quick, taking it all in.

BEFORE DINNER EACH EVENING, Caitlin practiced her driving. She and Mum took the loop by the vegetable garden with the windows rolled down. Lumbering down the rutted road, the station wagon would scrape its fender on the deep holes, making Mum wince. This evening after the race tea when Caitlin looked over, Mum's face was pensive. A few strands of hair were caught in the side of her mouth but she didn't brush them away. They drove by the pond choked with lily pads and high-blown weeds, and passed the fence Dad had made. He'd also built a hitching post at the parking place and when they rounded the corner they found it occupied. Tied up to it was a horse and carriage.

"Oh," said Mum, sitting forward. The glint in her eye showed that she knew the carriage, and well. It was one of the smaller carriages, with a black hood curving over a double seat, no windows. The horse's long face was close to the car, its blinders out like absurd shutters, staring at them. Further back, in the gray shade of the bonnet, they could see the back of Wilbur Kittredge's head and the silvery spot on it. Behind him, with a different glow, was a white T-shirt arching upward.

"Turn around," Mum said.

Caitlin shifted into neutral and the engine roared.

"Back up." Mum was looking everywhere but forward. The car went stuttering backward in jerks. Once around the corner, they stopped and switched places and Mum drove home.

The wind dies down at that time of day and the bay past Clam Cove, its mud flat shiny, was pearly and still, a silk tablecloth with sailboats sitting on top, motionless.

"I didn't think we should get any nearer," said Mum after a while. "Those are especially spirited horses. They spook." The crease in her forehead hinted at deeper knowledge. Whatever it was, she kept it to herself.

NOT LONG AFTER, THE island fell under the spell of a heat wave that wouldn't let up. It lasted for the rest of the summer. A limpid air hung over the glassy thorofare, which remained undulating and languid and pale blue. Screams and splashes could be heard day and night as kids ran drumming off the floats. Over the Labor Day weekend was the Kittredges' annual clambake, but the Vincents didn't go. Dad had played too long on the golf course that day and was out with heat stroke. He shut himself in his room, pulled the shades down, and lay in the dark. Mum, who sometimes went to parties without him, this year did not feel up to it and went to bed early too. At the end of the summer, the Vincents returned to Marshport and once again Wilbur

Kittredge's postcards appeared on the hall table—greetings from distant lands like Peru or Zanzibar or the Seychelle Islands—cheerful notes dashed off in a loose, large hand, unsigned.

The following spring, after her fortieth birthday, Rosie Vincent gave birth for the eighth time. It was a girl, Miranda Rose. Everyone was excited; there hadn't been a baby in the house for years.

Mum sat up in bed in her pretty nightgown, the pillows behind her bordered in *fleurs-de-lis*, holding her new treasure. Everyone hovered around, knocking against the dust ruffle, lying diagonally at her feet. Mum gazed into the infant eyes, seeing their strange clarity. She touched the tiny nose. She uncurled the fiddlehead fists and showed them to everyone lolling around. "You see?" she said. "Her father's hands exactly."

Then came the feeding. They watched her unbutton the nightgown and feel inside for the bosom. After fixing it to the baby mouth, and satisfied with it, she looked up. Caitlin and Sophie saw it—that wild look—only this time there was something added. It was aimed at them and it said: There is nothing in the world compares with this.

The eye was fierce. The baby stayed fast. There is nothing so thrilling as this. Nothing.

The Vocabulary of Absence

Helena Mulkerns

Helena

I HAD A DREAM of matriarchs. The cottage was small and dark, and in one corner, an elderly woman with mischievous eyes sat beside a fire, on which rested a small, bright copper kettle. She was indistinct in the shadows, but the steam off the kettle rose steady, and the whole room reflected rosily in the round copper surface.

In the center of the room, a woman, in her midthirties, with a gentle face and capable manner, was working at a wooden table. Several other women were bustling around another fireplace to her right. There was a sideboard on her left that had upon it, among other things, a dead rabbit and a laptop computer.

When the woman at the table looked up at me, I realized it was my grandmother, Ellen D'Arcy Quinn. The other women were my mother and aunts: Dolores, Eve, Ursula, Helen, and Madeleine. The elderly lady was, most likely, my great-great-grandmother Eliza, born in 1840.

My grandmother didn't speak, but she looked at me quite directly, with striking dark eyes. As I woke up, in my gray New York studio, I realized that her eyes had been communicating a very distinct imperative, that I should talk to my mother, Helen.

I remember E-mailing Mam about this dream, and noting that we should get together for a real chat, but it wasn't until Caledonia called me up requesting a piece for her new anthology that I actually had the perfect opportunity to do this.

I called my cousin Jackie Quinn, in Birmingham, England, who, for the last twelve years, has been researching the maternal side of the family. She sent me a thick pile of collated information detailing the family back as far as 1789. My second cousin, Gerardine Loughman in San Francisco, sent me a beautiful photo of our great-grandmother's gravestone, which I forwarded by E-mail to Helen, mentioning that *Motherland* had room for the story of a daughter who left and a mother who stayed—the experience of several generations of women in the family already.

Jackie's research revealed a fascinating mosaic of lives, both tragic and joyous. Take Ellen Delaney, born in 1848 and who, at around age nineteen, fell deeply in love with one John Armstrong, a young Protestant student from the North of England, over on vacation in Kildare. When the two announced their engagement (a Catholic Irishwoman and a Protestant Englishman), both families disowned them. They ran away to Dublin to live together until she was twenty-one and no longer needed her father's consent to be married. Four months after the wedding, our great-grandmother Mary Jane was born.

Then there was Eliza McGrath, our other great-great-grandmother, who married John D'Arcy on September 28, 1858. They had a baby which died at birth, while in the nearby manor house, Lord Carew's wife had also had a baby the same day, but the mother herself had not survived the birth. Lord Carew asked if Eliza would wet-nurse the motherless baby, and although she refused at first, she realized the baby would die otherwise, and so, twice a day, she would travel in the lord's carriage up to the manor house. As the child grew up, he looked upon her family as his own, until Lord Carew sent him away to boarding school. Eliza used to like a little drop of whiskey or poteen in later years and owned a small copper kettle in which she distilled the latter. It is now in New York City, the only "family heirloom" in my possession.

I left home for the first time when I was sixteen, to go and teach English in Spain. Since then, I have been "away" more than at home. At first, you don't stop to analyze your situation, because everything is so exciting and new. The sense that you may be missing the world that you uprooted yourself from doesn't develop for some time.

Communication with "home" can be deceiving. You try to be positive, so do those at home, dealing with the immediate, keeping up with the local gossip. No one likes to send bad news, and bringing up old ghosts can always be left until the next time. The visit home at Christmas becomes the annual, obligatory "catching up" stint, reserved for family and old friends. It's usually spent rushing around, drinking copious amounts of alcohol, and not spending enough time with anybody, least of all family.

When you then head back to Australia, London, New York, Munich, or Tokyo on one of those subdued, packed flights around the eighth or ninth of January, you're left regretting all the things you didn't say, all the questions unasked, the dreams unexpressed. You'll be lucky if you just about had time to meet everybody and "say hello."

Gradually, as the years go by, you become increasingly distanced, more emotionally than geographically. Home is just a plane ride away, but a million miles in terms of the reality of what you've missed out on "at home," whether it be important changes in your parents' and friends' lives or just the very necessary bond that makes a loved one real to you.

My mother, Helen, did not emigrate, choosing to stay in Ireland when it was experiencing an upturn in its economic fortunes in the sixties. She has remained there, with my father, and we have communicated down the years by letter, phone, and more recently via E-mail. I think I know her, and try to spend as much time with her as possible when I go home, but then again, when I leave, I always feel that it hasn't been enough.

I've always wanted to ask her what it was like for her, growing up in Ireland through the war and the fifties, experiencing the sixties (which she once described to me, late one night after one of her openings, as "the high point of the universe"). Occasional memories and half-forgotten stories are often not enough. We ended up having extended interviews, where I learned a lot about both her and where I come from, an exercise both enjoyable and fascinating.

My earliest memory of Helen is of her on a bright summer afternoon, in a turquoise dress, with her blond hair up in a funny chignon and smiling. Another involves a waft of Chanel No. 5, with her wearing a pale pink, embossed satin ball gown, leaning over my crib to kiss me good-bye when leaving to go out one night.

I still hate the smell of that perfume, presumably since it meant "Mother leaving."

I went through a period of rejecting my mother in my teens, so perfectly described in Mary Pipher's *Reviving Ophelia* that I gave her a copy of it to read, in a belated attempt at explanation. But since my late twenties, she has really become my best friend, and certainly the person with whom I'm in most regular contact, despite the distance.

Still, that funny look from my grandmother in the dream voiced what I "kept meaning to do"—that is, get a chance to sit down and speak with her. I know my mother, and yet I don't. She has always been a very kind and compassionate person but at the same time seemed to me to be often quite reserved, and conservative. As I've (or we've) grown older, however, I see her increasingly as tolerant and open-minded, with a certain innate charm that touches most people and an understated lust for life that keeps her spirit much younger than her age in chronological years. She has always encouraged anything I chose to do and never turned against me for mistakes I have made.

She refuses to acknowledge herself as a "feminist," which disappoints me, but then, all things considered, including our interview, I realize that she has basically lived her life, albeit in her own quiet, private way, as a feminist. She has gone against the grain in a number of ways and is now achieving one of her early aspirations, working as an artist, in watercolors and oils. We are in frequent contact on the Internet.

Absence: does the term sound less desolate as the world becomes smaller with our ever information-drenched, communication-complex society? Or is its vocabulary still, by default, a forced repartee, stemming from the fact that we often try to deny the distance is even there? We carry on regardless, as if the ache of missing someone is just not an issue.

I've been absent for a long time and have only recently begun to reflect on this. Somewhere between my grandmother's dreamlook and Helen and me sitting down to talk in spring 1998 in New York and Connecticut, it occurred to me that this was a chance to decode our tenuous vocabulary of absence—or at least make a beginning at doing so.

HELEN

MY MOTHER, ELLEN, CAME from a town called Athy, in County Kildare, which was the other side of the The Curragh from Kildare town. The main British Army barracks, where they bred all the horses, was on The Curragh. One of the stories I always remember her telling me happened during the Great War, when she would have been about thirteen, about the boys shipping off to the front out of Athy railway station. She was hanging over the bridge, in the very early morning when it was still dark, watching their departure.

In 1916 the Rising mostly took place in Dublin, and in the towns, but where she grew up the young men were part of a different tradition. If they weren't working on the farm, they might have joined the British Army, and that was life. A lot of her childhood friends would have gone off that morning, and she'd never have seen them again.

As she told it, the steam train was hissing and the noise of the engine was deafening. The horses were all banging their hooves, their brasses gleaming under the gaslight and the red glow of the train's furnace. The men were shouting and jostling in the smoke, and between the whole lot, she always said it was like a scene from hell: all the young men going off to the Somme, to their deaths. And the saddest thing of all was that they thought it was great. They only thought of the glory and honor of going to war.

Mammy came from a reasonably well-off family. David D'Arcy, her father, had a job as a steward on a big estate, which was solid work at the time. Like most families, many went away. My mother's sister Annie married a military officer named Sanchez and went to India. Her brother John went to teach in England and ended up as the headmaster of a large school in Essex. My own mother came up to Dublin to be a teacher but then met my father and got married. He came from County Tyrone and was involved with horses; there are a lot of old photos of him with horses, looking very smart.

They had their own stables for a while, while they were living in Cheltenham in England, which is a big horse-racing town. But they lost their money sometime in the midtwenties, when all the horses got some terrible disease and died. So they came back to Dublin and just worked their way through the thirties, and the war, and I know that there was never very much money.

I remember we used to go up to the Featherbed Mountain in County Dublin to cut turf for fuel during the war. Families were able to get a plot of bogland, and you'd go up on lorries run by private companies, crammed into seats in the back of the truck. You'd cut a load or two, and it might do you for the winter. There was a very wide expanse of bogland up there in the mountains, nothing between you and the sky for miles.

I was born in 1934, and in 1939–40 there was a big diphtheria epidemic in Dublin. I got it, and it was a very close call for a time whether I was going to pull through or not. I was in one hospital, and my sister Ursula was sick at that time too and in another. Every day in the papers, since there were almost no private phones then, they published the number of each child's bed in each hospital—so that parents and relatives could see how they were doing—bed number 456 was "improving" or was "very serious" or "dangerously ill," et cetera. Every hospital in Dublin was jammed. I remember being terrified, because I was next in line to go into the "iron lung," but I pulled through before they had to put me in it. A lot of children died that year.

I grew up on the South Circular Road in Dublin, in a place called Rialto—which had a lot of small houses, sometimes with fairly large families in them. At that time the countryside started just about two streets away from us. It was before the suburbs really started and Dublin was very small. When we were kids, my mother always wanted to take us out of the city to "go for a walk." We used to go to our "apple field" and our "daisy field" and there was another place where there was an old mill and a stream, and we used to try and jump over the rocks but were always falling in and getting wet.

There were two boys, five girls, and my mother and father. My second eldest brother, Donald, went to England to work during the war. The next time we saw him, he was married with a baby girl. During the war a lot of people emigrated to England, for employment in the munitions works and the factories. We were a neutral country, so trade was difficult, there was little work, and nobody had very much money. In the fifties it started picking up. That's when my father went into business on his own.

I went to school with the Sisters of Charity, in Basin Lane, which was an interesting part of Dublin, near the Liberties. When it came to secondary school, Mammy was quite ambitious for her daughters. She took myself and Ursula over to the Dominican College in Eccles Street, a famous school called Scoil Catriona, where they taught everything in the Irish language. A lot of very interesting Irish women went there, such as Margaret Burke Sheridan, Kate Tynan, Margaret McCurtain, and many more, because the Dominican nuns encouraged study of the arts.

There were a couple of fascinating women at that time in the convent, when I look back. One nun called Sister Aquinas was a powerhouse of energy—she sort of sailed along the corridors, her big bosom sticking out in front of her, organizing everything. Then there was another whom we all thought was absolutely beautiful, Sister Iseult. She was tall, and fair, and sort of floated along, and we all wondered why she entered the convent, because she was so lovely. We never found out, of course. You wouldn't, back then. But in the old days it was one of the few alternatives to the standard lifestyle. If they didn't want to get married and have children, often women chose the vocation.

When I left school in 1950, with a very good leaving certificate (high school graduation), I was only sixteen, because they had always put me in the A class, a year ahead of where I should have been, because I was a good student. I thought that was great, but what I didn't realize at the time was what a difference it was going to make in my life. Because with those high marks, I could have got a scholarship into the College of Art. But to enter, or to apply for the scholarship, you had to be seventeen years old. So my rushing ahead in the academic side actually put a stop to my getting into the College of Art, which I would have liked to do. So having done my leaving certificate, like most girls I did a secretarial course and got a fairly good job in the Civil Service. I didn't go back to study art until many years later.

As far as I was concerned, however, I was having a great time. Even when I was at work, I nearly always had some other outlet. I dabbled in various things like acting, modeling, and so on. I think people thought I was slightly crazy to do all that stuff, instead of just working nine to five and then going home to attend the novenas! I couldn't stand those kind of things.

When I decided to do modeling in my spare time, there were only about six or eight professional models in Dublin, and two agencies. I was with one, and my sister Eve was with the other. Even at the office during the week, I always managed to squeeze a few hours in for a modeling job, or a photographic session, so I never felt stuck in a boring day job.

I always had to be the "junior miss," because I was the smallest. What they called the *petite* model. I think the skinny, six-footer model thing came in very recently. It's very overrated, because how many women are six feet tall? Or as skinny as they look today? It's unrealistic.

The first date I ever had was when I was about fifteen or sixteen. We went to the pictures, of course, and then I went home. When you went out, you always went to the movies, or dancing on a Saturday night.

In terms of sexual freedom—or repression, whichever way you look at it—there was a certain general code of behavior, which seems no longer to exist. Although people talk about the fifties or forties as being a very restrictive period, at the time that code existed, in many ways, to protect women. I think that a lot of young men at that time just accepted that there were rules and regulations, and that you didn't do certain things. On the other hand, you can't pretend that it was perfect. If a girl got raped, she'd be disgraced, no matter if it wasn't her fault, she'd still be disgraced—"ruined" as they used to say.

I'd be inclined to think that the unfortunate downside to our liberation, and the availability of contraception (which was, of course, another huge step ahead) is that standards have dropped, and a lot of girls today don't even know how to respect or protect themselves. They see it as a great freedom, but you can still make your life awfully miserable. I wouldn't like to go back to the old days, but I think that some young women could do with more of a sense of that code today than they currently have.

Well, I managed to enjoy myself in the fifties, in any case. When I was seventeen or eighteen, I got to go to dress dances, where you wore long, formal-length dresses. They were always held in the big hotels with full dance bands. I just loved dancing.

People were beginning to socialize a lot more, the war was beginning to fade into memory. We were going to dances in town or local tennis club "hops" on a Saturday night, which were the big thing, where you went to meet fellows. Dixieland jazz, swing, and jive were all the rage. In the bigger ballrooms in the city you wouldn't be allowed to do that. You'd be tapped on the shoulder and asked to stop. But in the tennis clubs, you could bee-bop away, and the little groups at that time that used to play in the tennis club hops were great.

Rock 'n' roll was the next thing. My sister Ursula was away in Spain for a long time in the fifties, and she hadn't heard Elvis Presley, and so when she came home, I remember telling her, "Just wait till you hear this . . ."

That was around the time of my youngest sister, Madeleine's

twenty-first birthday party. I was going out with Jim and had gone to drama school, and so I was doing some acting. I played Nora in *The Plough and the Stars* at one point, and I did the summer season—summer stock—for a couple of years, with the occasional part in larger Dublin productions.

For example, I was in the Mac Liammóir-Edwards production of *Julius Caesar*, A.D. 57. It set the great Shakespeare play in a contemporary fascist state. The soldiers wore storm trooper uniforms, and the back of the stage was lined with huge flags, like at the Nuremberg rallies, that kind of thing. I was one of the "rabble" who ran on and offstage shouting at set moments. Just at the end of Mac Liammóir's "Friends, Romans, countrymen . . ." speech, the crowd, roused up, was supposed to cheer and create a riot onstage before running off. As we did so, somebody in front of me knocked down a flagpole, and all I could see was this great big flagpole and flag billowing down in the direction of Mac Liammóir's forehead.

So I grabbed it. And of course, you should never do anything on a stage unless you've rehearsed it. Because then what do you do with the bloody thing when you have it in your hand? The rest of the rabble was rapidly disappearing out through the wings, and there I was, with that flagpole. Quick as I could, I drove it hopefully back down into its base and flew. All went well, anyway, and nobody was too much the wiser. I only told him years later at a party in the Arts Club, and he just said, "I thank you very much, my dear. I never knew that!" He was quite a character.

I was introduced to Jim Mulkerns at the National Union of Journalists Ball. He was just about the most unusual person that I had ever met. Or in fact that most people who knew him had ever met. He had jet black hair, was very handsome, with pronounced eyebrows and a huge, RAF mustache, which came out so far that you could practically see it from the back. He was a very flamboyant character; he had a passion for classical music and film. He rang me up the next day, sent me flowers, tried to give me a gold wristwatch!

Everybody said, "Don't take a wristwatch from a fella, he must be after something! Girls don't accept gifts from someone they only met the night before." So I followed their advice, and he said, "Okay, I'm not giving it to you now, you'll have to ask me for it when you want it."

He was the best theater photographer in Dublin. He did all the actors' portraits, Mac Liammóir, Hilton Edwards, Siobhán McKenna, and more. And he did the theater front-of-house photographs.

I had great fun going out with him, because we went such different places. Through him I met all the theater crowd, and the newspaper crowd. I'd go with him on assignments, all over the country, at the weekend. Once, when my mother thought I was at work, he took me up in a two-seater plane, and we flew over our house from up above and took photos of it. It was all very exciting and new. After a year, I said, "I'll take that watch now." We went to Paris for our honeymoon.

You were born practically in the most famous after-hours bar in Dublin, Groomes Hotel at the top of O'Connell Street. It was a highly respectable shebeen where all the actors went, judges, politicians, et cetera. We used to go there most nights. I didn't actually drink, because I couldn't drink or eat when I was pregnant. But I never stayed at home, ever. Like that night—we left Groomes at about three in the morning, and we were on our way to the hospital about an hour and a half later!

I never believed in being the little "stay-at-home" wife. I saw so many girls who got married and disappeared, and you never saw them again. You just didn't see them around. They just drifted into motherhood and the housewife role, and after a while they had no personalities left, they'd no anything left. That was it. They had accomplished their goal in life, which was to get married and have kids, whereas I always wanted more.

For instance, we only had two children. That was a decision. I didn't think it was a great deal of fun for anybody, including the kids, if you had six of them to look after. My mother never brought it up, but I'm quite sure she knew exactly. She had seven herself and would have thought I was being sensible, probably.

I no longer had my Civil Service job, of course. As soon as you got married, you had to leave. You got a certain grant of money when you left, a "marriage gratuity," which was probably deducted over the years as you worked anyway.

That was all settled in the 1920s and thirties, with De Valera. Even though women were supposed to be equal, like it stated in the Irish Proclamation, various bills were passed to keep them "in the home." The early Irish suffragists, like Hanna Sheehy-Skeffington or Louie Bennett, and those women who had been involved in nationalism, fought the bills, but they were defeated.

And when you grew up with that, you just sort of accepted it. The ordinary woman when I was growing up took it as a matter of course that when you got married, you didn't usually go out to work. It would have been almost impossible to get a job, for a start. Most didn't feel all that deprived, except one in a few. If you wanted to do something else then, you did it on your own. It didn't stop some people.

A lot of girls went to America, or England. I had one good friend who went off to Florida to be a nun. One day she told me her plan, and to be honest, I was a bit skeptical about her *vocation*! But anyway, off she went to America to be a nun! Whether she stayed in the convent or not, I don't know.

Once you were married, there was no going back. Divorce only came in a couple of years ago. To massive opposition, needless to say. There was still a certain extremist antidivorce faction who were predicting that the minute divorce came into Ireland, the courts would be full, as if it would be obligatory to get divorced just because it was available. They never seemed to be able to accept the fact that just because divorce was available didn't necessarily mean that every second woman was going to be looking for one. In fact, even after it came in, there were relatively few divorces. It's still not something people do lightly.

Anybody of my age, though, would tend to stay together as long as possible. It was just something you were brought up with. When you're married, you're married to the one person. Obviously, there were some women who were married to the *wrong* person. But if they had kids they just stuck together. Sometimes the husband would go to England to get a job and send the money back. I suppose there were a lot of men, too, who regretted who they married. I'm sure it works both ways.

I heard of families where the mother and father didn't talk to one another at all. It was difficult to understand. Then over the years things began to break down a little, so that people got separated, and they'd leave and maybe go and live with somebody else.

You could eventually get a legal separation, but it was very difficult—and still socially unacceptable.

But when I got married, I was actually quite happy to give up the boring office job. We went out and bought some lovely furniture with the marriage gratuity! I continued doing a bit of modeling, or acting, and in a way I never did "stop working," really, because after that I worked in the film business with Jim, which I always enjoyed.

After working as a photographer, Jim was working for the Irish Tourist Board and became involved in the film section, making travelogues. This was part of the development of the Irish film industry. At the moment, there is a huge boom in Irish film, but back in the early sixties the "film business" was very small, and people didn't even sort of think of there being one. There was nothing like the Irish Film Board or the Arts Council to give grants to filmmakers. It wasn't considered an "art" as such, like theater or literature, and wouldn't be for many years.

Jim then started working in the newsreel business, which was the most popular form of visual news before television, distributed every week to all cinemas around the country. It was the first all-Irish newsreel ever, produced by Colm O'Laoghaire, who was well-known in the documentary film industry. Jim was the cameraman, and his assistant was Val Ennis. It was financed by the Irish language organization Gael-Linn, which was a corporation that promoted and encouraged the Irish language. So the newsreel was shot and recorded entirely in Irish Gaelic, which provided a great alternative at the time to the only other newsreel available in Ireland, Pathé News, which was a British-based outfit that rarely included material on Ireland itself.

But although I worked in film down the years, it couldn't really have been construed as working full-time. It wasn't like now where you'd have a positive career, and you'd train to do one thing like be an editor or a producer. The way we worked, everybody did a bit of everything.

We were also involved with the Irish Film Society, which had been founded in 1935, by Liam O'Laoghaire, as a reaction to the censorship laws which had been brought in by the state. Some people used to think that censorship just meant cutting out the "sexy bits" in films, but in fact they banned a lot of films which contained political material that went against the conservative government as well. None of the great Russian films were allowed in the country, for example. No Luis Buñuel, nor much of the French New Wave, et cetera. The film society were true students of cinema, they elevated film, respected it, and showed movies that could not be shown anywhere else in Ireland.

In the sixties, things were good. Jim and I never emigrated, because we wanted to try and make a go of things in Ireland, although it wasn't a particularly political decision. I had fun when you were small, with you and your brother, Doug. I had a friend who lived nearby with a little boy the same age as you, so the two of us would frequently meet up and go out with the prams. Since we lived fairly close to the seaside as well, in summer we used to take the two of you to the beach and spend the afternoon there.

After the newsreels, we made documentaries, and did advertising. When television started we made the first ads that ever appeared on television in Ireland. It was fun. We also made a lot of government-sponsored films, which was really the only source of financing at the time. One of the most successful was *An t-Oilleanch*

a d'Fhill (The Return of the Islander), which was shot on the Aran
Islands and won an award at the Cork Film Festival in 1970. We
lived on the Aran Islands during the time that was being filmed,
which is how you went to school in a native Irish-speaking environment for a time.

Sometime during the seventies, I went back to study art, because
I had always liked it. I had a little bit more free time as you kids were
growing up, then, and I didn't have a full-time job at that stage. So I
went back to art classes in the College of Art in Dun Laoghaire, and
then I decided to go back to work. You can get very bored hanging
around all day in your house, with the kids at school. I got work
teaching art in boys' private school, which was great at first, but I
quickly discovered that I preferred actually painting to teaching art.
So when I got an opportunity to work in public relations, it suited
me much better.

I would work (as I always did, I suppose) during the day, and
paint for pleasure nights and weekends. Eventually I got together
a collection of paintings and gave my first exhibition in a recognized gallery in Dublin. It was very successful for somebody who
hadn't exhibited before, and I was amazed that people wanted to
buy the paintings; it was very nice to be successful in that field. At
that time I was only painting in oils. I painted a lot of old city
scenes around Dublin city itself, because I was always interested in
that.

After another exhibition, and selling paintings from various gal-
leries in Dublin, I opted for what I'm still doing today. A regular
open-air exhibition of art was set up in a square in Dublin opposite
the National Gallery of Ireland, so I joined that, and it has turned
out very well. Selling directly to people at an outdoor exhibition

is very pleasant. You are independent, and you get to meet people and talk to them about your painting. I've had quite a few commissions from individuals and large corporations, so my work is hanging in quite a few places now. I've sold a lot to people from abroad. That's mostly what I'm doing now, and I hope to continue for a long time to come.

I've painted in all different parts of Ireland, a lot in Connemara and the West or South. Mostly, I prefer to work from a combination of my own photographs and small sketches, so I can capture the angle and the light that I want, and then develop it in my studio. I don't try to do large watercolors on the spot, because the weather doesn't always allow for that in Ireland!

I also work in the publications office of a worldwide religious order in Dublin which is active in the field of mental health and psychiatry, compiling our staff newsletter and other publications, doing layout, computer graphics, research, and photography. Recently we've done a book on the history of St. John of God, and I've been helping to set up our home page on the Internet, which has meant learning a lot of new things.

The best thing about the Internet, from my point of view, is the E-mail system. If half the mothers in Ireland knew how to use it, and had the equipment, they'd be on the E-mail all day long! I find it invaluable. It's sad, really, because there was a period in the seventies where people started to actually come back to Ireland, and a feeling that emigration was over. But it was a sort of false optimism, because there was another exodus of young people again in the eighties—the so-called Ryanair or green card generation. The difference there was that they weren't, most of them, just going off to build roads.

Years ago, the Irish built the train tunnels in Scotland, and the motorways in England, when all the building started up after the war. A lot of them were very unhappy—out of their depth, and lonely. In the eighties, young people were more educated, self-confident, and had started moving around the world. You still had the young fellows that built the Channel Tunnel, but you also had the college graduates making their careers in the software industries and the new European financial markets.

You were a part of that wave, I suppose. I often feel that I missed out a good deal when you went away, because, for instance, my mother was always my adviser and companion in all sorts of ways, we were very close. And when you left, I felt I missed out on the kind of companionship that mothers and daughters have on a simple everyday basis. Sometimes it's just the little things that you miss—shopping trips, walks, coming home to the kitchen in the evening and going over what might have happened during the day.

The first time you went away, I really felt very grieved, if you like, when you went off on that boat at Dun Laoghaire. I remember thinking at the time how awful it was to think of your daughter going off, and you were very young—and although I knew you were coming back, I remember reflecting on what it must have been like when people went off to America years ago, and everybody knew that they were never coming home. It was no wonder they called the good-bye ceremonies American wake.

When you decided to go, which was when you left school, I was very sad, but I didn't want to stand in your way. You were very determined. I feared that had you stayed, your ambition could have been dampened, you might have turned out a different person. And I suppose, in a feminist sense, if you like, I wanted to give you all the opportunities possible.

Nowadays, of course, the opportunities for women are vastly different, much better. It's not to say that we haven't had some very tough times for women over the last couple of decades, what with the struggles over the abortion and divorce referendums, the X case, and more. I have never belonged to an organized feminist group, but I have always kept up with political developments and used my right to vote. My idea always was that underneath everything, my mother, too, would have been a suffragist. She always stuck up for women, and, for example, she paid great attention to our education. When my father died, she ran the business by herself for a few years, and she engaged one of the few woman barristers to look after the legal aspect of things.

What's encouraging is that, in the past couple of decades, we have seen the number of women in Irish politics triple. We have women TD's (members of parliament); ministers of state; our current tánaiste (the second in command in the government) is a woman; and of course, our former and current presidents are women: Mary Robinson, who is presently high commissioner for human rights at the United Nations, and Mary McAleese, currently in power. In business and management, sport, the arts, women have been making enormous strides. In fact, the only place where they have not made progress is in the Catholic Church!

Another sad landmark, of course, was the first Christmas you were away. We missed you a lot then. That's one thing about emigration, it's the feeling of expecting to share a certain section of your life with somebody, and yet suddenly, they're gone, and you're missing that experience. That hit me pretty hard. And I never really wanted to say too much about it, because you don't want the person who's gone away to feel that they've made you upset. I would never have said to you in a letter, "I'm very sad, I'm very miserable that you're gone," and all the rest of it, because I felt that then you'd feel responsible for that.

This in a way, relates to your idea of "The Vocabulary of Absence," which definitely exists. Because when you are communicating with someone who is far away, you instinctively edit what you are saying, into a form that softens the message. You lose the urgency of immediate contact, and the sting of the message is blunted. Although I said the E-mail is a great thing, it can still be deceiving. Some people use it very superficially, zapping one- and two-liners back and forth over the Web and nothing more. If you are a good writer, you may have time to think things over. But the danger with instant communication is that of saying too much too soon—so you learn to be cautious in what you say—an extension of that vocabulary.

In the fifties, when a lot of people I knew were leaving, I didn't go. The expression "to take the boat" became ingrained in the Irish mentality like a curse, because whereas some wanted to go, for most it was a necessity—to get work. Two of my sisters, Dolores and Eve, went, and my brother Donald. It's a strange thing, but I find, as time goes on, that I miss them, too, more and more.

I would, of course, have liked to spend more time with you, and hope to be able to in the future. But on the other hand, let's be realistic. If we had lived next door to each other over the last twenty years, we might not have ended up such good friends.

FROM *Living Out Loud*

ANNA QUINDLEN

IN THE BEGINNING

IT WAS VERY cold the night my mother died. She was a little older than I am today, a young woman with five young children who had been eaten alive by disease, had wasted away to a wisp, had turned into a handful of bones wound round with pale silk. When my father came home from the hospital we gathered the younger children in his bedroom and tried to tell them what had happened. Naturally we could not; it would be years before we would know ourselves. Perhaps it is some indication of how spectacularly difficult our task was, and how spectacularly we failed at it, that, when we were both adults, my younger sister told me that she had spent five years waiting for our mother to come home from the hospital, where she was certain they would find a way to make her well.

I suppose this is an odd way to begin the story of writing a column of personal reflections, a column that I did not start to write until a full fifteen years after the January evening on which my mother died. And yet it is the beginning. For there are two parts to writing a column about yourself, about your life and your feelings. One is, naturally, the writing itself, the prose and, if you've got it in you, the poetry.

But the other is the living, and that is the harder part. When I was twenty-two, I wanted badly to do such a column, but the managing editor of the newspaper for which I was working said that I was a good enough writer, but that I hadn't lived enough to be qualified for "living out loud." At the time I was enraged by his attitude; now I know he was right. My prose may have been adequate, but my emotional development was not.

It was not until the aftermath of my mother's death that I began to realize that I would have to fashion a life for myself—and that is what I have been trying to do, in a workmanlike way, ever since. This seems rather ordinary to me now, but at the beginning it was odd and frightening. Up until that point life had fashioned me. There had been almost no decisions for me to make, in part because I was not permitted to make them, and in part because I saw no path other than the one I was on. I went to school, did well, came home, ate dinner, finished my homework, went to bed. I fought with my brothers and loved but did not know my parents. I wore what my friends wore and said the kinds of things they said, and if, somewhere, someone was deciding what we should wear and discuss, I did not know who that someone was. There were two good reasons not to interfere with such a life. I felt powerless to do so, and I was happy.

It was a lucky coincidence for me that this impeccable super-structure and my own private frame of reference came tumbling down at about the same time, since I like to take all my medicine at once rather than have it doled out in dribs and drabs. My mother began to die on the cusp of the sixties and the seventies, at the same time that the religion and the rules that had circumscribed her life and mine died, too. And I was left with a self to do with what I pleased. I felt as though someone had handed me a grenade with the pin pulled.

Now I know that I was one among many, that all over America and indeed the world women were beginning to feel this same way, beginning to feel the great blessing and the horrible curse of enormous possibility. "Oh, you girls," an elderly woman once sighed, talking to me of my job and looking down at my belly big with child as we sat together in a nursing home in New York City. "All these choices for you." I smiled, and she sighed. "I feel so sorry for you," she added, and I smiled again, for I knew she was right.

I knew that in the years following that January night I had been numb with fear at some simple truths: that I was going to have to find a way to earn a living, make a decision about what I wanted to do and how to go about doing it, find a home and make it my own. That was the only response I could find to the scent of death, sticking to my clothes, rising from my hair. The house in which my mother had sickened and drawn near to death was sold not long after she died, and so in every sense I was adrift. I felt orphaned, cut off from the past. It was many years before I would know that I had found both feelings liberating.

It was perfectly valid to feel adrift. There were few role models. The women of my mother's generation had, in the main, only one decision to make about their lives: who they would marry. From that, so much else followed: where they would live, in what sort of conditions, whether they would be happy or sad or, so often, a bit of both. There were roles and there were rules. My mother did not work. The money she spent was earned by my father. Her children arrived as nature saw fit. I assumed that she never used birth control, although when I was eighteen she set me straight. "Yes, we did," she said. "Rhythm."

My father often says today that he believes their marriage would have been sorely tried by the changes which became my birthright. And I think he is right. When I was younger and saw the world in black and white, I believed the woman my mother was was determined by her character, not by social conditions. Now that I see only shades of gray, I know that that is nonsense. She would have gotten her second wind in the seventies. She would have wanted the things I have come to take for granted: work, money, a say in the matter, a voice of her own. She would have wanted to run her life, too. Instead she was born and died in an era in which her life ran her.

I have rarely felt that way about my own life. I have mostly felt free to do and be what I wish, and I have felt compelled to analyze endlessly what and who that is. I would like to be able to say it is because I am a thoughtful and analytical person, but this is not true. It is because, in the hard and selfish way in which—usually covertly—the living view the dead, I realized after my mother died I was salvaging one thing from the ruin of my life as I had known it. And that was that I was still alive. I know now that on some unconscious level somewhere in the long and gray months left in that horrid winter, I determined I was going to squeeze every bit of juice from the great gift of a beating heart within my body.

It was only coincidental that, not long after my mother died, I found an unusually safe way to do this. I had wanted to be a writer for most of my life, and in the service of the writing I became a reporter. For many years I was able to observe, even to feel, life vividly, but at secondhand. I was able to stand over the chalk outline of a body on a sidewalk dappled with black blood; to stand behind the glass and look down into an operating theater where one man was placing a heart in the yawning chest of another; to sit in the park on the first day of summer and find myself professionally obligated to record all the glories of it. Every day I found answers: who, what, when, where, and why.

But in my own life, as I grew older, I realized I had only questions. For a long time this made me feel vulnerable and afraid, and then suddenly, as though I had reached a kind of emotional puberty, it made me feel vulnerable and comfortable. It is too easy to say that this great change came about when I had children, although having them, discovering that the meaning of life is life, trading in the indelible image of my mother swollen with death for one of myself big as a beach ball with possibility, certainly contributed to the change. What was more important was that I finally realized that making sense of my life meant, in part, accepting the shifting nature of its sands. My religion changing, one step forward, two steps back; my marriage always in a state of re-creation and refinement; my children changing constantly, as children always have: I had nothing but questions. It was terrifying and fascinating.

One of the most exhilarating parts of it was that my work became a reflection of my life. After years of being a professional observer of other people's lives, I was given the opportunity to be a professional observer of my own. I was permitted—and permitted myself—to write a column, not about my answers, but about my questions. Never did I make so much sense of my life as I did then, for it was inevitable that as a writer I would find out most clearly what I thought, and what I only thought I thought, when I saw it written down. I suddenly knew that at some point in the fifteen years since that cold winter night, I had come back from the dead. I knew it because, after years of feeling secondhand, of feeling the pain of the widow, the joy of the winner, I was able to allow myself to feel those emotions for myself.

I had often felt alone with these feelings because of the particular circumstances of my own life. But over the last two years, as I wrote my columns and read the letters they evoked, I realized more and more that what has happened to me has been typical. A kind of earthquake in the center of my life shook everything up, and left me to rearrange the pieces. Similar earthquakes were felt round the world, precipitated not just by the deaths of people but by the demise of rules, mores, ways of living and thinking. As the aftershocks reverberate, I have had to approach some simple tasks in new ways, and so have the people who have read what I have written. Looking back at my past. Loving my husband. Raising my children. Being a woman. It is no accident that each of those tasks is couched in the present participle, that lovely part of speech that simply goes on and on and on. Oddly enough, what I have learned since that January night many years ago is that life is not so much about beginnings and endings as it is about going on and on and on. It is about muddling through the middle. That is what I am doing now. Muddling through the middle. Living out loud.

The Need to Feed

CAROLYN RAMSAY

My grandmother grew senile when she was in her late seventies and cataracts clouded her eyes. She would sit on our living room couch, her hands busily working a rosary and tissue, her brow creased with worry about images on a television screen she could barely see.

"There's a man at the window," she'd call blindly in a thin voice. "Will someone make him a sandwich? He's hungry."

My grandfather and I would catch eyes and he would slap the air with annoyance, as if to say, "Don't listen to her." When no one responded, she'd lean forward to heave herself from the sofa. "Let me get him something to eat."

My grandfather would grip his arm around her shoulder and pull her back to the sofa, scolding: "God bless us and save us, Mother. There's no one at the window. Just sit down."

This happened over and over, several times a day, confusing

and alarming my nine-year-old self. The image of a head at the window frightened me. I couldn't understand my grandmother's impulse to feed someone lurking in the alley. What if he were a robber or murderer? If you fed him, wouldn't he just keep coming back? I finally asked my mother what my grandmother meant and she explained that during the Great Depression, hungry men walked the alleys of West Philadelphia begging for hand-outs.

"My mother always gave them a sandwich or some leftovers," she said. "We were poor but she always found them something to eat."

It might also have had to do with the fact that her parents emigrated from a country where over a million of the people had starved to death, but that was never mentioned.

The memory of my grandmother, in the confused last days of her life, pushing herself blindly off the couch for the sole purpose of feeding an imagined hungry man left a profound impression on me. Either because of her powerful modeling or on the twisted threads of heredity, I acquired my grandmother's urge to feed people. When the soup kitchen where I once worked asked me to write a recruitment letter, I wrote about my grandmother. I've donated holiday turkeys, money and clothing to another soup kitchen and fed hundreds of people in my home each year. I've fiddled with a short story about a gourmet soup kitchen and fantasized about planting fruit trees in poor neighborhoods to create a ready supply of fresh, nutritious food.

These are not the typical pre-occupations of professional women with families in Los Angeles. I don't know another working mother who worries about feeding people the way I do. My friends either don't cook at all or have full-time maids to prepare family meals. It has taken me years, on the other hand, to learn to focus on just feeding my family—not the entire world.

On late nights when I've pounded chicken and chopped vegetables alone in my kitchen while my family sleeps, I've wondered what precisely my problem is. I've always associated it with my Grandmom Duffey, but she also carried a heavy pocketbook filled to the brim with pennies and I don't hoard money. Part of me passes off the feeding urge as a slightly embarrassing compulsion, although its emotional depth and power indicates otherwise. After dropping food at a soup kitchen for the first time a decade ago, I had to steer my car to the side of the street because I was sobbing so hard that I couldn't see. There's such unremitting sadness at the root of this drive to feed people that I've come to assume that it links me somehow to the dark events of Ireland in the mid-1800s.

I can't know this. No famine stories made their way from my migrating great-grandparents to me, or even to my parents. "The Irish aren't real talkers," my mother once said. When I consider how my grandmother's need to feed an imagined ghost has followed me for thirty years though, it seems likely that her famine-surviving parents' attitudes toward food made a deep impression on her. How could they not?

When I think of my grandmother before the cataracts and senility, I picture her always standing in her tiny kitchen, shredding cabbage with her soft wrinkled hands, asking over and over if everyone had had enough to eat, or reluctantly slicing bruises, the bad spots, from a banana for me. "When I was a girl, we called them the good spots," she'd say, gently admonishing my wastefulness.

Although my grandmother was born in Philadelphia, her parents were both from Ireland. Their migration stories are beautiful and mythic, blessed with the Irish gift for romance and optimism. Even before telling the first one, my mother said she doubted its veracity. "I'm sure the reason I'm American is because of the Famine," she said.

The story goes that my grandfather's mother was from an upper middle-class Dublin family and fell in love with a fisherman named James Duffey. Her parents didn't approve, so they sent her to a proper Catholic boarding school in Philadelphia to make her forget him. James missed her so much that he sailed his fishing boat all the way across the Atlantic to marry her.

My grandmother's mother told stories of a happy childhood in Kells, County Meath, where she mischievously picked apples from trees around the famous monastery there and threw them at the praying monks. She too emigrated for a man she loved, she told my aunt, and never saw her family again. Neither Irish woman ever even mentioned the Great Famine or its devastating aftermath to their grandchildren. There was nothing about difficult journeys on creaking ships that are part of most American migration stories. It was almost as though leaving one's family and country were necessary sacrifices for love.

The stories must be interpreted in the context in which they were told, of course. While baby-sitting their grandchildren, these Famine-era women answered the inevitable questions about their lives. It would be natural to romanticize, wouldn't it? Children are so serious and impressionable; a grandmother knows that.

What little I know of my mother's family's Famine experience is a treasure trove compared to what I know about my father's family. My sister spent years studying our ancestry at the Library of Congress in Washington, DC, but could never find the Ramsays' point of immigration. Ramsay is a Scottish and English name but my father joked and sang with a mimicked Irish brogue. We always considered ourselves Irish, exclusively, and Catholic. We identified with the Irish persona of tough, inner steeliness cloaked in charm. The Kennedys personified the American version of the archetype; I was named for Caroline.

The facts and stories I know of my family don't explain my grandmother's emotional need to feed people or mine. Since I was a teenager cooking spaghetti dinners for my brothers, I've fed hundreds of people in my home and in the soup kitchen. I've grown hundreds of vegetables and handed them out to friends and neighbors. The summer I was pregnant with my son, I grew enough vegetables for a family of ten and stocked the pantry until cans of soup, tuna and fruit spilled out when you opened the cupboard door. I did this even though the quick mart a block away was open all night.

We have two refrigerators in our home and both are always packed—plates of lemon chicken rest precariously on jugs of milk and boxes of cake. Friends come to my house and head straight for the refrigerator, even when they have no intention of eating. They want to see what treats are inside. At the moment, there are brownies baked from scratch; fresh peaches, cherries, grapes and plums; homemade cranberry, ginger and peanut sauces in jelly jars with peeling labels; six loaves of bread, five cartons of ice cream and forty bottles of soda. There's far too much food for this household of three spaghetti-thin people: my husband, seven-year-old son and myself.

My friends, I worry, think I'm either showing off or suffering such low self-esteem that I feel chained to the kitchen. "Stop it with the cooking, will you? You're making me look bad," a friend said the other day. I was embarrassed. I couldn't articulate my compulsion about feeding people and worried maybe I was showing off. It seemed ridiculous to tell her food is sacred to me.

When I fantasize about what I'd do if I were rich or powerful, as every American does, I don't think about buying a fancy car or a mountain retreat. I honestly wonder how many orange, pomegranate and persimmon trees I could plant along the streets of this sunny, fertile city. That way, hungry people could eat without the shame of begging. One day, I was obsessing about the trees and who would care for them and whether I could set up a system whereby the poor could harvest the fruit and sell it on street corners in Beverly Hills. I was apparently talking at such a pitch, my husband finally said gently, "Don't worry, honey. You'll do it. You'll make it happen."

When I read articles about American businesses abandoning inner city neighborhoods, I predict that old factories and industrial plants will be razed or destroyed and replaced by squatters' farms. I have not read of another person predicting such a fanciful outcome.

This deep empathy for the hungry comes from a woman whose life can be characterized only as abundant. There is something about hunger in particular that calls to me in a way that ordinary empathy for orphaned children, handicapped old people or endangered animals does not.

When I saw Jim Sheridan's movie *The Field*, I believed I found the causal link between my grandmother, our mutual obsession and me. The character Bull McCabe makes a speech about the Famine scattering his people "to the four corners of the Earth." I stopped breathing when I heard that. I felt a nervous, pit-of-the-stomach resonance of truth suddenly revealed. I was sure my ancestors had fled Ireland because of the Great Famine, that they had found prosperity and, because of guilt or sadness, needed to feed the hungry. I carried this belief even though I knew nothing of their stories.

Now that I've heard the stories, I'm frustrated. If they were so happy and prosperous there, why did they leave Ireland? Is it possible a sensitive child could pick up vestiges of survivor guilt unspoken by generations not inclined to gab about a devastating event? My great-grandparents, who were born in the 1860s, were obviously affected by the Great Famine but chose not to recall their memories for their grandchildren. To formidable old women in a bustling city and new country, it may have seemed like a distant piece of hard history they had been lucky to escape.

It's also possible that the Famine endures in the Irish collective unconscious, the way the Holocaust in Germany resides within Jews who have never experienced anti-Semitism. It's a wound on the Irish psyche that still aches, is still not healed. We each may interpret it differently, based on our experience. Because of my grandmother, I want to feed the hungry.

When I mentioned to friends of Irish ancestry that I was writing this essay, each told a story. One said her affluent mother always prepared too little food for her family—six chicken legs for a family of seven, for example—so that each dinner began with a scramble for food. Another friend's Irish-American grandmother limits herself to tea and so little food that she must occasionally be treated for malnutrition. She does this despite a full bank account. That friend dreams of creating a meal-cooking co-operative for nursing mothers who are too tired to prepare the nutritious nightly dinners that their bodies crave.

Many of us have obsessions about food that, due to the long silence about the Famine, we've struggled to comprehend. Americans believe so strongly that they create their own destiny, apart from their families and culture, that the Great Famine probably seems remote and insignificant to many. That the stories are being told now is a gift to us. It was a story of the Famine that helped me to make sense of my urge to feed people and give it a proper place in my personal mythology. For that I'm grateful. In the sudden spate of media regarding the Famine, the image that hit me hardest was not of starving children or crumbling poor houses, but of grassy hillsides divided by grey stones in the tiniest of plots, plots that once supported entire families for a year.

That image moved me, although not as powerfully as the memory of my grandmother pushing herself blindly off the couch to feed an imagined hungry man. I can't know my family history, can't fully understand why that memory haunts me so. In the insistent need to cook, carry plates to a full table and find food for the hungry, I sense a truth though. I believe it's the same impulse that haunted my grandmother at the end of her life, so each night, I let it pull me to the stove.

FROM *The New Motherhood*

MARGARET HIGGINS SANGER

THE GOAL

WHAT IS THE goal of woman's upward struggle? Is it voluntary motherhood? Is it general freedom? Or is it the birth of a new race? For freedom is not fruitless, but prolific of higher things. Being the most sacred aspect of woman's freedom, voluntary motherhood is motherhood in its highest and holiest form. It is motherhood unchained—motherhood ready to obey its own urge to remake the world.

Voluntary motherhood implies a new morality—a vigorous, constructive, liberated morality. That morality will, first of all, prevent the submergence of womanhood into motherhood. It will set its face against the conversion of women into mechanical maternity and toward the creation of a new race.

Woman's role has been that of an incubator and little more.

She has given birth to an incubated race. She has given to her children what little she was permitted to give, but of herself, of her personality, almost nothing. In the mass, she has brought forth quantity, not quality. The requirement of a male-dominated civilization has been numbers. She has met that requirement.

It is the essential function of voluntary motherhood to choose its own mate, to determine the time of child-bearing and to regulate strictly the number of offspring. Natural affection upon her part, instead of selection dictated by social or economic advantage, will give her a better fatherhood for her children. The exercise of her right to decide how many children she will have and when she shall have them will procure for her the time necessary to the development of other faculties than that of reproduction. She will give play to her tastes, her talents and her ambitions. She will become a full-rounded human being.

Thus and only thus will woman be able to transmit to her offspring those qualities which make for a greater race.

The importance of developing these qualities in the mothers for transmission to the children is apparent when we recall certain well-established principles of biology. In all of the animal species below the human, motherhood has a clearly discernible superiority over fatherhood. It is the first pulse of organic life. Fatherhood is the fertilizing element. Its development, compared with that of the mother cell, is comparatively new. Likewise, its influence upon the progeny is comparatively small. There are weighty authorities who assert that through the female alone come those modifications of form, capacity and ability which constitute evolutionary progress. It was the mothers who first developed cunning in chase, ingenuity in escaping enemies, skill in obtaining food and adaptability. It was they also who attained unfailing discretion in leadership, adaptation to environment and boldness in attack. When the animal kingdom as a whole is surveyed, these stand out as distinctly feminine traits. They stand out also as the characteristics by which the progress of species is measured.

Why is all this true of the lower species yet not true of human beings? The secret is revealed by one significant fact—the female's functions in these animal species are not limited to motherhood alone. Every organ and faculty is fully employed and perfected. Through the development of the individual mother, better and higher types of animals are produced and carried forward. In a word, natural law makes the female the expression and the conveyor of racial efficiency.

Birth control itself, often denounced as a violation of natural law, is nothing more or less than the facilitation of the process of weeding out the unfit, of preventing the birth of defectives or of those who will become defectives. So, in compliance with nature's working plan, we must permit womanhood its full development before we can expect of it efficient motherhood. If we are to make racial progress, this development of womanhood must precede motherhood in every individual woman. Then and then only can the mother cease to be an incubator and be a mother indeed. Then only can she transmit to her sons and daughters the qualities which make strong individuals and, collectively, a strong race.

Voluntary motherhood also implies the right of marriage without maternity. Two utterly different functions are developed in the two relationships. In order to give the mate relationship its full and free play, it is necessary that no woman should be a mother against her will. There are other reasons of course—reasons more frequently emphasized—but the reason just mentioned should never be overlooked. It is as important to the race as to the woman, for through it is developed that high love impulse which, conveyed to the child, attunes and perfects its being.

Marriage, quite aside from parentage, also gives two people invaluable experience. When parentage follows in its proper time, it is a better parentage because of the mutual adjustment and development—because of the knowledge thus gained. Few couples are fitted to understand the sacred mystery of child life until they have solved some of the problems arising out of their own love lives.

Maternal love, which usually follows upon a happy, satisfying mate love, becomes a strong and urgent craving. It then exists for two powerful, creative functions. First, for its own sake, and then for the sake of further enriching the conjugal relationship. It is from such soil that the new life should spring. It is the inherent right of the new life to have its inception in such physical ground, in such spiritual atmosphere. The child thus born is indeed a flower of love and a tremendous joy. It has within it the seeds of courage and of power. This child will have the greatest strength to surmount hardships, to withstand tyrannies, to set still higher the mark of human achievement.

Shall we pause here to speak again of the rights of womanhood, in itself and of itself, to be absolutely free? We have talked of this right so much in these pages, only to learn that in the end a free womanhood turns of its own desire to a free and happy motherhood, a motherhood which does not submerge the woman, but which is enriched because she is unsubmerged. When we voice, then, the necessity of setting the feminine spirit utterly and absolutely free, thought turns naturally not to the rights of the woman, nor indeed of the mother, but to the rights of the child—of all children in the world. For this is the miracle of free womanhood, that in its freedom it becomes the race mother and opens its heart in fruitful affection for humanity.

How narrow, how pitifully puny has become motherhood in its chains! The modern motherhood enfolds one or two adoring children of its own blood, and cherishes, protects and loves them. It does not reach out to all children. When motherhood is a high privilege, not a sordid, slavish requirement, it will encircle all. Its deep, passionate intensity will overflow the limits of blood relationship. Its beauty will shine upon all, for its beauty is of the soul, whose power of enfoldment is unbounded.

When motherhood becomes the fruit of a deep yearning, not the result of ignorance or accident, its children will become the foundation of a new race. There will be no killing of babies in the womb by abortion, nor through neglect in foundling homes, nor will there be infanticide. Neither will children die by inches in mills and factories. No man will dare to break a child's life upon the wheel of toil.

Voluntary motherhood will not be passive, resigned, or weak. Out of its craving will come forth a fierceness of love for its fruits that will make such men as remain unawakened stand aghast at its fury when offended. The tigress is less terrible in defense of her offspring than will be the human mother. The daughters of such women will not be given over to injustice and to prostitution; the sons will not perish in industry nor upon the battlefield. Nor could they meet these all too common fates if an undaunted motherhood were there to defend. Childhood and youth will be too valuable in the eyes of society to waste them in the murderous mills of blind greed and hate.

This is the dawn. Womanhood shakes off its bondage. It asserts its right to be free. In its freedom, its thoughts turn to the race. Like begets like. We gather perfect fruit from perfect trees. The race is but the amplification of its mother body, the multiplication of flesh habitations—beautiful and perfected for souls akin to the mother soul.

The relentless efforts of reactionary authority to suppress the message of birth control and of voluntary motherhood are futile. The powers of reaction cannot now prevent the feminine spirit from breaking its bonds. When the last fetter falls, the evils that have resulted from the suppression of woman's will to freedom will pass. Child slavery, prostitution, feeble-mindedness, physical deterioration, hunger, oppression and war will disappear from the earth.

In their subjection women have not been brave enough, strong enough, pure enough to bring forth great sons and daughters. Abused soil brings forth stunted growths. An abused motherhood has brought forth a low order of humanity. Great beings come forth at the call of high desire. Fearless motherhood goes out in love and passion for justice to all mankind. It brings forth fruits after its own kind. When the womb becomes fruitful through the desire of an aspiring love, another Newton will come forth to unlock further the secrets of the earth and the stars. There will come a Plato who will be understood, a Socrates who will drink no hemlock, and a Jesus who will not die upon the cross. These and the race that is to be await upon a motherhood that is to be sacred because it is free.

Contributors

CAROLYN CURTIN ALESSIO is deputy editor of the *Chicago Tribune* book section and editor of *Las Voces de la Esperanza:* a bilingual anthology of writings by the children of a Guatemalan squatter village.

ELLIN MACKAY BERLIN (1903–1988) was married for more than sixty years to songwriter Irving Berlin. She wrote for *The New Yorker* and published four novels; the first, *Land I Have Chosen*, was sold to Hollywood for what was then a record sum. Her last novel, *The Best of Families*, was published in 1970.

MADELINE BLAIS is a Pulitzer Prize–winning journalist and author of *In These Girls Hope Is a Muscle*, which was nominated for the National Book Award, and is a professor at the University of Massachusetts, Amherst.

MAEVE BRENNAN (1917–1993) came to the United States from Ireland at seventeen. She worked at *The New Yorker* for most of her adult life and contributed fiction and prose to the magazine. Her short fiction recently returned to print with the collection *The Springs of Affection*.

MARY CANTWELL worked in the magazine industry for many years. Most recently she was an editor at *The New York Times Magazine*. *Manhattan, When I Was Young*, which is excerpted here, is the second in her trilogy of memoirs.

LISA CAREY holds degrees from Boston College and Vermont College. Her first novel, *The Mermaids Singing*, chronicles three generations of Irish American women. She divides her time between the United States and Ireland.

KARIN COOK is the author of *What Girls Learn*. She graduated from Vassar College and New York University. She lives in New York City, where she is an activist and a health educator.

MARY DOYLE CURRAN (1917–1981) was born in Holyoke, Massachusetts. She was trained as a maid and ultimately received a master's from Iowa State University. A college professor, she taught at Wellesley and Queens Colleges and the University of Massachusetts, Boston.

M.F.K. FISHER (1908–1992) is the author of countless essays and writings, including *The Art of Eating* and *Among Friends*. She lived in both the United States and France and eventually settled in the wine country of northern California.

ELIZABETH GURLEY FLYNN (1890–1964) was a labor activist and organizer and the head of the American Communist party. A well-known orator, she spent her life fighting for the cause of labor and the poor. Her speeches have been published as well as her auto-biography, *The Rebel Girl*, where she writes about losing her only son.

DORIS KEARNS GOODWIN won the Pulitzer Prize for history for *No Ordinary Time*. She is a widely respected historian and biographer. Her books include *The Fitzgeralds and the Kennedys* and *Lyndon Johnson and the American Dream*. She appears on television frequently as a political commentator and lives in Massachusetts.

MARY GORDON's most recent novel is *Spending*. She is the author of *Shadow Man*, a memoir about her father, and is a well-known novelist. She has received a Guggenheim Fellowship and in 1996 she received the O. Henry Award for short fiction. She teaches at Barnard College and lives in New York City.

MARY HARRIS JONES, aka Mother Jones (1830–1930), was born in Cork, Ireland. She is considered the mother of the American labor movement and was one of the founders of the IWW. A fighter and activist, she lost her husband and all four of her children to a fever epidemic.

KERRY ANNE HERLIHY holds degrees from the New School for Social Research and the University of Massachusetts at Amherst. She lives in Brooklyn, New York, and teaches in a welfare-to-work program in Manhattan.

MAUREEN HOWARD's most recent novel is *A Lover's Almanac*. She has been publishing fiction for forty years. Her memoir, *Facts of Life*, received the National Book Award. Most recently, she received the Academy Award from the American Academy of Arts and Letters.

JEAN KERR is the author of several plays and many collections of her writing. She was widely published in women's magazines; her books include *Penny Candy*, *Please Don't Eat the Daisies* and *How I Got to Be Perfect*.

ROSEMARY MAHONEY's second book, *Whoredom in Kimmage*, is a collection of essays about a year she spent living in Ireland. Her most recent book, a memoir, *A Likely Story: One Summer with Lillian Hellman*, was published in October 1998.

MARTHA MANNING is a clinical psychologist and the author of two collections of nonfiction as well as a memoir, *Undercurrents: A Life Beneath the Surface*.

SUSAN MINOT is the author of three novels and a collection of short stories. Her first novel, *Monkeys*, received the Prix Temina in France. She wrote the screenplay for Bernardo Bertolucci's *Stealing Beauty*. *Evening* is her most recent novel.

HELENA MULKERNS, Irish born and raised, is a freelance journalist and fiction writer who has been widely anthologized in Ireland, the United States, and Australia. She is a founding member of the Irish Women Artists and Performers Collective, BANSHEE (www.banshee.com).

ANNA QUINDLEN is a Pulitzer Prize–winning columnist and novelist. Her most recent book, *Black and Blue*, was selected by Oprah Winfrey for her book club. Her second novel, *One True Thing*, was made into a major motion picture.

CAROLYN RAMSAY is a writer and journalist whose work has been published in many newspapers and magazines, including *People* and *The New York Times*. She lives in Los Angeles with her husband, Andy Goodman, and their children, Daniel and Olivia.

MARGARET HIGGINS SANGER (1879–1966) was a pioneer of the birth control movement and founded Planned Parenthood.

Permissions

CALEDONIA KEARNS is the editor of *Cabbage and Bones: An Anthology of Irish American Women's Fiction*. A graduate of the University of Massachusetts at Amherst, she lives with her husband and daughter in Brooklyn, New York.